Executive Summary

Got a minute? That's all the time it'll take you to check out this big little book . . .

- **First, skim the Contents on page 5.** That will take all of 15 seconds. You'll get the gist of the Creative Corporate Writer system. You'll see ideas you'll want to apply next time you write a report, an e-memo, a news story, a piece for a journal — *anything you write*.

- **Next spend 15 seconds on the CC Writer's Ideal** for Reading Ease on page 48. You'll find five goals to shoot for in your writing and editing. Five numbers to help you measure words, sentences, active voice, and two types of scales for for reading ease. You'll want to copy them onto a 3-by-5 card and take them to work so you can try them right away. Even today. Yes, today. This stuff isn't rocket science, after all.

- **Spend 20 seconds paging through the bold text** and figures in the rest of the book. First you feel the soul of the Creative Corporate Writer system. Then you begin to feel a need to use the system. Am I right?

- **So go to page 101** and dip into the CC Writer's bag of 101 tricks for a measly 10 seconds. Can't wait to get going, can you? So, what's keeping you?

Congratulations! You're on the way to becoming . . .

The
**Creative
Corporate
Writer**

www.creativecorporatewriter.com

Nonfiction by James V. Smith, Jr.

The Creative Corporate Writer — Infinity Publishing
You Can Write a Novel — Writer's Digest Books
The Fiction Writer's Brainstormer — Writer's Digest Books
Compelling — The Road to Best-Selling (Due in 2003)

Workshops and Services by James V. Smith, Jr.

The Creative Corporate Writer — Seminar
The Executive Writer — Seminar for Corporate Leaders
Compelling Corporate Writing — Consultations
Compelling — The Road to Best-Selling — Advanced
  Workshop in writing both fiction and nonfiction books
  for commercial markets
Write Your Novel — Basic Fiction Workshop

Visit *creativecorporatewriter.com* on the Web

The Creative Corporate Writer

JAMES V. SMITH, JR.

www.creativecorporatewriter.com

Copyright © 2003 by James V. Smith

ISBN 0-7414-1470-8

Published by:
INFINITY
PUBLISHING.COM
519 West Lancaster Avenue
Haverford, PA 19041-1413
Info@buybooksontheweb.com
www.buybooksontheweb.com
Toll-free (877) BUY BOOK
Local Phone (610) 520-2500
Fax (610) 519-0261

Printed in the United States of America

Printed on Recycled Paper

Published April 2003

Contents

i Let's talk about you 7
What this book can do for you.

The 10 Suggestions

1. Focus – Make your bottom line the top line 17
Cut to the chase. First tell *what* you want, then *why*.

2. Focus on the *You*, a single reader and his hot button 29
Feed your reader's most basic need: *It's all about me.*

3. Focus on a single aim, either to compel or to inform 41
Think before you write—one minute to settle four issues.

4. Focus on the Creative Corporate Writer's Reading Ease Ideal 47
Meet five writing goals, and you'll boost reading ease.

5. Focus your edit on writing short words 73
Steal the secret of best-selling authors and use it at work.

6. Focus your edit on writing short, tight sentences 87
Cut the fat, even in high-tech writing.

7. Focus your edit on writing just one topic in each paragraph 89
Use white space to your advantage.

8. Focus your edit on writing in a polite, informal style 91
Avoid a bossy tone, please, even if you are the boss of me.

9. Focus your reader with stories and pictures 93
Appeal to the visual and sensory reader in each of us.

10. Focus – Organize for clarity 95
Lay out your case with a system that makes sense.

ii The Creative Corporate Writer's bag of 101 tricks 101
Get it right. Avoid the common errors in corporate writing.

iii A Final Word (or three) 109
Three mega-suggestions that say it all to the CC Writer.

Index 111

It ain't art, it's bidness
— From *You Can Write a Novel*

For every kid sent to the board and made to write
sentences as punishment by Sister Blister of
the Holy Order of the Inquisition.

For every corporate writer drowning in the trench-
es filled with the detritus of
FWD:FWD:FWD:CC:BCC, and copy-and-
paste-copy-and-paste-copy-and-paste.

For every memo-writer who thinks she must open
a vein just to tell the staff to stop setting their
coffee cups on the tops of
computer monitors.

For every boss so schizo about legal action that
the invitations to the company party read like
the historic Roe v. Wade Supreme Court
decision.

Take heart.
Stop sweating it.
Writing is so-o-o simple.
I'm about to show you how.
All together now. A deep breath.
Let it out. Look to *Chapter i*. Let us begin.

James V. Smith, Jr.
Shelby, Montana
April, 2003

i

Let's talk about you

As a Creative Corporate Writer, you can gain a huge edge over your peers in pay, promotions, sales, and career success. A company full of CC Writers will slay the competition. And it's so simple. CC Writers follow a one-word CC Writer Commandment and The Ten Suggestions. The word is *Focus*, which tells you what to do. The Ten Suggestions tell you how. All without using the G-word, *grammar*. All without trying to turn you into a literary giant. That's what this chapter's all about, what this book's all about.

What this book can do for you

This book will give you, the person, an edge on your peers. It will give you, the company, an edge on your competition.

You, the person

This book will help you cut junk out of your writing. It will help you make your words twice as effective in half the space. You will stand out because your writing stands out.

This book will change your life — your writing life, mostly. But also your business life and your financial life. With this book in your hands you have taken the first step on your road to becoming a truly Creative Corporate Writer.

Is this your all-too familiar problem at work?

How many times have you lived this story . . . ?

A guy at work stops you in the hallway and asks, "Where's that meeting again?"

"Room 101," you say.

"What time again?"

"Three o'clock." As you're thinking, *I put it in the memo, bonehead. Didn't you read the memo?*

Question: Whose fault is it, really, when the guy doesn't read your memo?

Answer: Maybe you're right — maybe the guy is a bonehead. On the other hand . . .

What if the guy snags you in the hall because your words don't snag him at his desk? What if nobody reads your stuff because it's too dense. Or worse, they don't think it matters.

Solution: This book can help you get people to read what you write. From now on, you can make your writing matter.

You, the company

Imagine the real-dollar savings you could achieve if every memo, e-mail, and tech report did not waste words. How much time and money would your firm save if every written piece was 50 percent shorter and twice as powerful? Your staff would spend less time writing and much less time reading and re-reading. Your prospects would have less trouble seeing the path to becoming customers. Bosses would get to the point in a memo, and their staff members would know exactly what the boss's point was. Report writers could write concise material. If only, right? If only they knew how.

They can. This book can teach your people — all your people, from sales staff to clerks to secretaries to PR pros to managers — how to write straight to the bottom line.

That's the competitive edge. As a Creative Corporate Writer, you can beat the competition. You can beat the curve.

You remember the curve from school, don't you?

We call it the bell curve. It shows the normal pattern of test scores. Teachers use this pattern to assign grades from A to F.

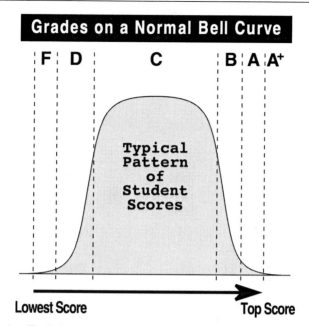

Figure 1 — The bell curve showing the normal pattern of grade distribution.

On every test, a small percentage of student scores will fall at either end of the scale. Those at the far left get the grade of F. Those on the right, no matter what their actual score, get an A, with maybe an A+ to the top 1 percent of super-students who always get extra credit.

Most scores fall in the middle. Those scores earn a C grade. B and D grades fall between the extremes and the middle.

Now let's apply the bell curve to corporate writers. In place of test scores, let's use writing competence.

If you gave 100 corporate writers the same set of facts and told them to write a memo, the results would vary in writing quality. If we graded those memos, the scores would fall into the same bell curve pattern you learned in school.

Some writers would write a superb memo; others would write pure junk. Most efforts would fall into that wasteland of the ordinary, boring, and unread. Here, I've assigned grades and descriptions of the work you'd see from either Creative Corporate Writers or everybody else. Like this . . .

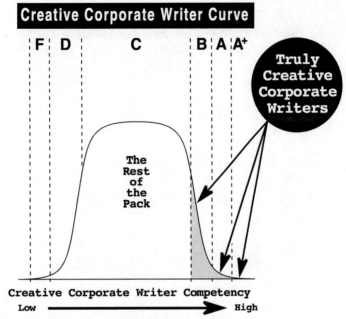

Figure 2 — The bell-curve of corporate writers.

Creative Corporate Writers

CC Writers share many traits. They write clear, compact messages. They interest you. They get to the point. They are polite. They take their work seriously, but they don't take themselves too seriously. What they write is easy to read, easy to grasp. You keep a file of what they write. Because you need it, because you use it, because it's flat too good to throw away.

The three grades of CC Writers

A+ for the Superstar. The Superstar CC Writer writes clear, effective material. She's a natural talent, a closet poet.

A for Excellent. The Excellent CC Writer doesn't have the genius style of the Superstar, but is every bit as effective with words and ideas. He shows flashes of Superstar status.

B is for the Brilliant CC Writer. This writer gets the job done with the fewest number of words. She takes pride in her writing, and it shows. Even if she doesn't write Superstar prose, her words sparkle with clarity.

Everybody else in the world of corporate writing

The rest of the pack writes ordinary stuff. They turn simple messages into aimless junk. You avoid reading this junk, if you can. You skip passages. You tire of searching to find the bottom line. You follow up with a phone call or a face-to-face, maybe snag them in the hall. All in all, bad news.

The good news about this bad news?

- You don't have to go far to get to the next level, from ordinary to Brilliant or even higher on the scale. You can be a Creative Corporate Writer with modest talent and earnest effort. Best of all . . .

- You don't have to re-take high school English. And you don't have to be a literary genius. You don't even have to break a sweat.

- All you have to do is follow . . .

The one-word Creative Corporate Writer Commandment:

FOCUS

I've studied government and corporate writing for decades. With a tool I'll teach you to use, I've analyzed books, memos, ads, articles, e-mails, and Internet Web pages. Here's what I found: More than anything else, *the* fatal flaw in today's corporate writing is lack of focus. Too many and too much. Too many words, too many ideas, too much strain, too much nuance. In short, too little focus.

So the rest of this book focuses on focus. I'll tell you how and why to focus your words, sentences, paragraphs, and ideas. I'll teach you some nifty tricks you can use in putting more focus into your corporate writing. From now on, your readers will get more out of what you write. Using . . .

The 10 Suggestions

1. Focus — Make your bottom line the top line.

2. Focus on the *You*, a single reader and his hot button.

   3. Focus on a single aim, either to compel or to inform.

   4. Focus your edit on the Creative Corporate Writer's
      Reading Ease Ideal. To achieve this ideal for compact
      writing, edit using Suggestions 5 through 8 . . .

   5. Focus your edit on writing short words.

   6. Focus your edit on writing short, tight sentences.

   7. Focus your edit on writing just one topic in each para-
      graph.

   8. Focus on writing in a polite, informal style.

   9. Focus your reader with stories and pictures.

   10. Focus — Organize for clarity.

Put these Ten Suggestions to work and you'll be a truly
Creative Corporate Writer. What's more, you'll have the tools
to judge your own writing and the work of others. If you want
to teach the CC Writer system in-house, use this book.

Now, as to the other side of the coin . . .

What this book will not do to you

   • It will not bury you under a load of grammar rules.

   • It will not try to turn you into a literary genius.

Simple as that.

What creative corporate writing looks like

I'll let two real-world samples speak for me. Here's a memo
from a typical company.

A typical before-memo

```
Subject: Salary Increase Web Forms

Good Morning,

With the perpetual changes that we are all
faced with as managers, we thought that this
would be a good time to review a few things
that will not be changing in 2002.
```

> For managers with final salary approval, we
> are requesting that all salary increase Web
> forms be submitted to the SALVO box no later
> than the 15th of the month prior to their
> effective date (SATELLITEDIV send Web forms to
> the SATVO box). This will help to ensure that
> we are able to complete our review of the
> request, as well as allow the HR Service
> Center to process and input the request by the
> 1st of the month. Please confirm the appropri-
> ate cut off date with your next level of man-
> agement within your area of the SATELLITEDIV
> organization. In the event that you have
> extenuating circumstances around the need for
> a salary change that extends beyond the 15th
> of the month, we can review on a case by case
> basis until the end of the month prior to the
> effective date.

And now for the after-memo, meaning . . .

After a Creative Corporate Writer edited the memo:

> Subject: How to submit salary increases
>
> Good Morning,
>
> Your salaries mean a lot to us. So let's
> review how to submit pay changes for your
> staff. That way, paychecks will get out on
> time and in the right amount.
>
> Please submit pay change Web forms by the 15th
> of the month. This will help us get changes
> made for you before the first of next month.
>
> If you need to make a change after the 15th,
> do get in touch. We can often help you right
> up until the end of the month.
>
> If you're in SATELLITEDIV, run your Web forms
> by your boss first to confirm the cut-off
> date. Then send it to the SATVO box.
>
> All other Web forms go to the SALVO box.

You don't need me to tell you the large-scale difference
between the two memos. You can see the difference in densi-
ty without reading a word. Then, if you do read a few words,
you'll see for yourself there's a difference in quality as well
as quantity.

As to the details, I used nine of the Ten Suggestions to edit
the first version into the second. All in less than 10 minutes.
I'll refer to these two pieces from time to time, so you can see
some of the craft that went into the revision. It's not literature.
It's not poetry, to be sure. But it does have a sparkle of elegant

clarity to it, wouldn't you say? It also has a high-level of readability, something we'll talk about in detail in Chapter 4.

So. We have to follow only one commandment: *Focus*. All else in the Creative Corporate Writer system is based on it.

I'm speaking of the 10 Suggestions, of course. Let's get to them, shall we?

Chapter summary

You can rise above your peers using Creative Corporate Writer methods. Your company, if it packs its staff with CC Writers, will rise above its competition. Why? Because you will become reader-friendly. Clients, customers, and prospects won't have to struggle to read your messages. How do you do this? Focus. It's as simple as that, using the 10 CC Writer Suggestions. No grammar, no lessons in literary prose. All in fewer than 112 pages.

The 10 Suggestions

I call them Suggestions. Not rules or commandments. They are all you need to know about writing on the job, in a few pages, without reliance on the rules of grammar, without some writing coach trying to turn you into Tolstoy. Visual tools to help you in the pre-writing stage. A scale to help you judge the readability of your work and the work of others. Techniques to help you edit your own work so you can become . . .

The Creative Corporate Writer

1

Focus–Make your bottom line the top line

Tell your reader *what* you want, then *why* and *how*, not the other way around. A simple trick can help you focus on just what you want — set a 15-second deadline. When you can, put your bottom line in the subject line.

Cut to the Chase

Once upon a time, I was reading a bedtime story to my daughter, Jill. *The Three Bears*, for the hundredth time. At the chair-too-hard, chair-too-soft part, Jill taps me on the arm, her eyes shut, and she says:

"The bears, Dad. I'm tired. Get to the bears."

Good advice, corporate writers: *Cut to the chase.*

Write the result you want. Forget the setup, background, and logic that lead up to a result that follows. Say the result first. Then explain the *why* and *how*.

True, fiction plays best when you fill it with suspense. And, yes, fairy tales get their charm from elaborate setups and repetition.

Not so on the job. There you write for a purpose, either to compel some action or to inform.

Yet how many times have you tried to follow the logic in a company memo about why something should be done without knowing what it is that ought to be done?

A VP at a major national firm insisted I address this issue in a workshop for her people. "The thing that irks me most," she said, "is to get a message, usually an e-mail, with a dozen attachments at the bottom and a dozen references at the top. The writer starts off referring to our phone calls, my memo, the CEO's policy, the company SOP, and five other bits of background. I read and wonder, *Where is this thing going?* I feel like I'm in voice-mail-hell where the operator gives me nine options, *If you wish to make a buy, press one*— all the way down to ten. Then I get to the end of the message, and he didn't give me the choice I want."

The problem? That's right, a lack of focus.

How does this VP handle such material?

"I send it back," she said. "I tell the writer, *If you can't tell me what you have to say in 50 words, I don't want to read it.*"

Know what I think? This VP is ahead of the curve in corporate writing. Still . . . the 50-word limit to her patience is far too generous. She might double her effect on the staff by cutting her patience in half, to 25 words.

Still, the number of words is not so critical as how you use those words. An example.

Remember that memo in Chapter 1 from a typical company? Here's the first text graf of the original memo:

```
With the perpetual changes that we are all
faced with as managers, we thought that this
would be a good time to review a few things
that will not be changing in 2002.
```

The problem? Friendly as they are, the opening lines of the memo do not even hint at the topic the writer will address.

This intro says, *You must keep reading to see what I'm talking about.* I have two words for that: No fair.

And the fix? Just get to the point.

```
Your salaries mean a lot to us. So let's
review how to submit pay changes for your
staff. That way, paychecks will get out on
time and in the right amount.
```

My edit is a mere two words shorter. But my 31 words say a ton more than the 33 of the before-version. They say:

- The topic is *salary*. Now all by itself, *salary* is a word that goes *cha-ching!* Words like *pay*, *money*, *salary*, and *free* do get people's attention.

- The memo will review the steps to submit pay changes, then tells why it's important.

- Good things will happen for managers who follow the steps, namely, paychecks will be right.

- The writer cares about how you look to your staff.

When you read the revision, you know the topic and where the writer is going. This intro says: *Stay tuned for details.*

The main purpose of the memo is to inform. The writer shrewdly gives incentives to compel managers to comply. Without using any threats, the memo implies, *We'll bend over backward to help out. But if you screw up this simple SOP, your people will blame you for not getting paid on time.*

Many company memos try to compel readers in more direct terms. They try either to order, persuade, or sell something.

What better place to study such a directive that tries to give an order than the U.S. Army?

The Memo from Never-Never Land

Read this Army directive, an order. Read it as if it were from your boss giving you a command to do or not to do. The letter seems high-tech-military, but you need to know only two things: A rotary wing aircraft is a helicopter; and an autorotation is a power-off emergency landing by a helicopter.

```
Subject: Aircraft Safety
To: All 20th Aviation Division Rotary Wing
    Pilots

Per longstanding Federal Aviation
Administration (FAA) policy, Department of
Defense Logistics Command (DoDLC), XXIII
Corps, this headquarters, local directives and
recent events at the airfield facility here at
Gratuitous Army Airfield, it is imperative
that existing standing operating procedures be
suspended to take into account Modification
```

Work Orders (MWOs) not yet applied due to the backlog of UH-1H rotary wing aircraft fleet modifications already underway. In particular, safety considerations currently in effect have proven inadequate in the prevention of a singular catastrophic occurrence peculiar to the UH-1H.

On multiple recent emergency procedure qualification flights, the landing gear strut braces have failed due to unforeseen metal fatigue in the UH-1H landing apparatus. As a consequence, the multiple resultant aircraft mishaps accumulated a total of more than three million dollars ($3,000,000.00) in damage to government property and the loss of an estimated one hundred fifty seven (157) man-days. Fortunately, only the expertise, experience, and readiness of the involved instructor pilots minimized damages and possibly curtailed loss of life.

The incidents in question, including one catastrophic mishap accompanied by a near-fatality, occurred during the practice of the maneuver known as the running landing, usually undertaken during a concurrent hydraulics-off emergency procedure.

Therefore, these circumstances mandate a temporary suspension of high-friction maneuvers involving prolonged moving skid contact on asphalt, concrete, and dirt landing surfaces.

Specifically, all running landings and autorotation maneuvers terminating with skid-to-ground contact are suspended until further notice from this command. Autorotations must be terminated with full engine recovery BEFORE fifty (50) feet Above Ground Level (AGL). Running landings are prohibited altogether, (altitude notwithstanding and under any circumstances.)

Once pending skid MWOs have been applied (and adequately tested by competent authority as designated by this headquarters or higher), the aforementioned procedures may be resumed, but once again, only by this command, on notice exclusively from the undersigned.

Pilots failing to abide by the explicit instructions of this directive will be prosecuted to the fullest extent under the Uniform Code of Military Justice (UCMJ).

Subordinate commanders notify each UH-1H-qualified aviator and reply by indorsement to that effect.

(Commanding Officer's Signature)

The directive is fiction, based on an actual piece. But, hey.

You've seen memos like this one on your job, too.

When you read a piece like this, if you can bring yourself to read it at all, what happens?

Sure, your eyes glaze over at some point in the first graf, probably in the whopping 66-word first sentence. You want to stop reading, but if you're a pilot, you can't. So you begin to skim. You look for clues like *therefore* in the fourth graf and *specifically* in the fifth graf. You skip to the last graf, where you might expect to find the literal bottom line.

But the bottom line is not at the bottom, is it? The bottom line lies buried under big words in the fourth and fifth grafs, after all. Now you have to go back and re-read a piece you didn't want to read in the first place. *Arrrgh!*

Can you say the bottom line in one breath? Do it. Yes, now.

Got it? How would you rewrite the piece to move that bottom line to the top line?

If you want to give it a try, go ahead. I'll rewrite it the way I would if I were still in the Army.

Revised Army Memo

To: All division UH-1H pilots

Subject: Running landings and full-contact
         autorotations prohibited UFN

Stop all running landings and full-contact
autorotations as of today. The skids could
break off and cause you to crash.

You may still autorotate but you must make
full engine recovery at 50 feet above ground
level or higher.

Once we inspect and repair the fleet, I will
give the all-clear for the return to normal
ops.

Commanders, get this word out to every UH-1H
pilot in your unit. Let me know when you've
done so, please.

(Commanding Officer's Signature)

The edited Army piece deals with dozens of CCW issues. The first is length. The edit cuts the memo from 344 words to just 77. That brevity alone makes the bottom line easier to identify. But let's discuss other points that pertain to the issue of putting the bottom line at the top.

First and foremost, the piece . . .

• **Compels**, or as they say in the Army, gives orders. As the first order of business, the edited piece gives orders to UH-1H pilots and to commanders of those pilots.

The first graf says to stop the two types of skid-to-ground landings as of today, the date of the memo.

The second graf further tells them to recover from autorotations at 50 feet above the ground or higher.

The last graf tells commanders to get the word out and to report when they're done. The piece also . . .

• **Informs.** In the second sentence, the edited piece tells why pilots must stop making skid-to-ground landings: *You might crash.* The third graf tells what must happen before the boss lifts the ban. It also says, *I'm the guy who says so.*

You ask: *Is that all?*

Sure. What else do you need?

You counter: *What about all the elaborate info, the references, background, the losses in dollars, the threat under the UCMJ, the military's legal system?*

Junk, all junk. Junk that gets in the way of the bottom line.

You might argue that all that other stuff needs to be in the piece, that you would add it to the end.

I say, it's junk. Leave it out.

Think about it. What is the point of this Army memo? To get pilots to stop making two types of landings, right? Why add the clutter?

Hey, this is a life-and-death matter. We're talking crashes. If I'm the boss, before anybody else gets hurt, I want to say: *Stop doing things that lead to crashes.*

Give people credit. They don't need as much as you think. In that first memo, the writer needed to protect himself. He was on a mission to close every legal loophole. He wasn't writing to the UH-1H pilots. He was writing, not to relay orders and info, but to cover himself on paper. That's why the reader needed a seeing-eye dog to interpret the memo. For

Pete's sake, it wasn't written for pilots; it was written for the writer and for all his bosses in the military chain of command.

The second memo does its job without all the junk that gets in the way of the central message.

Don't take my word for it. Just ask yourself how long it took to figure out the bottom line in the first memo.

Compare that to the time it took to get the point of the second memo. That's your clue, your bottom line clue. Get it?

Yeah, but would it stand up in court?

I hear you. You think you have to cover your butt on paper or else the lawyers will eat you alive in a lawsuit. Face it, you could write every company memo as long and detailed as a flood insurance policy and still not deflect every basis for court action.

Say, did you see the TV news item a while ago about Farmer Bilko who set up and used a ladder in a barn? He found a secure footing on a pile of frozen manure. That worked fine in winter, but in spring, the manure thawed, the ladder fell, and the farmer got hurt.

You guessed it, Farmer Bilko sued the ladder maker for not having a sticker on the ladder to warn him about the dangers of standing it on frozen manure that might later thaw.

Now ladders in that brand have labels warning of manure thaw, and they must work. To date, no more cases of manure-thaw injuries have gone into court.

I assure you, even if that ladder had had a manure-thaw label, Farmer Bilko and her lawyer would have found a different cause for action.

I also assure you, you can't cover every loophole in every memo. Nothing in the Army's before-memo will bulletproof it against the rare idiot who can't or won't read. Or any other loophole finder put on earth to vex you in front of a judge.

Hey, that first memo won't stand up in court any better than the revision. At least in the new piece, the message is direct. At least the 99 percent of non-idiots can decipher its main point on one reading.

Perhaps the direct tone of the second piece will give pause to the loophole finder. Maybe it will make her stop and think: *This boss, she doesn't write like a person who debates shades of gray.*

You still want warning labels? Here's a warning label:

> Don't write down to the idiot in your firm. Don't spend 99 percent of your effort covering your tail against the 1 percent of your people who might make trouble for you. Take a stand. Show some grit.

Adding junk to a memo is little more than a sign of insecurity. Adding a threat betrays insecurity to the point of neurosis. Enough said. Let's move on to your other concerns.

It's so blunt

I can see your point. No beating around the page, just saying what you want to say. As they say in the mob movies: *You gotta problem wit dat?*

Being clear is what separates the CC Writer from the crowd. What you call blunt just seems so because it is so clutter-free, so simple, so direct, so rare.

Yeah, but it's so informal

Yep, even conversational. It doesn't taste like the bane of original writing, copy-and-paste jargon.

In most companies, people borrow bad writing from the last guy. They look for a memo on the same topic from last week, then copy huge chunks into the new memo. Trouble is, the old memo stole from the week before, all the way back to when Abner Old Guy founded the company.

Forget about what Abner would have said. Do your own words get the job done? Great, then use them.

Be a CC Writer. Reflect on the situation. Apply your own ideas. Your own emotions. Your own good thinking. Give it your own touch. Give it new life.

What's my bottom line?

Good question.

It's one thing for me to throw up some bad examples, hunt down the bottom line, and move it up to the top line. Before you begin fresh on a new e-mail, memo, or report, how do you identify your own bottom line?

Here's how, using a little trick. I call this tool . . .

15-Seconds to the Bottom Line

That's all it takes, a lousy 15 seconds. Picture this. You have a memo to write to your staff. You sit at the keyboard and that little cartoon creep appears in a pop-up window.

The cartoon creep hijacks your computer screen like the terrorist he is. He sends you this message:

> I'm your worst nightmare, a computer terrorist more vicious than any worm or virus you have ever seen. You now have 15 seconds to type the bottom line to that memo you're working on and send it to the printer. At the end of 15 seconds, start running, because I'm about to blow up your computer.

Now here's the trick:

> Imagine that scene and spend the 15 seconds each time you sit down to write. Your bottom line will come to you. Type it. You're on your way to CC Writer superstardom.

If you don't type it, at least say it to yourself. And another thing . . .

> If you want to get the most out of this tip, hit the stop-watch function on your wristwatch and time yourself. Or bring a kitchen timer to work and set it for 15 seconds, start the clock, then go on and get to your bottom line. Just say to yourself: *Before my computer blows up in 15 seconds, what do I want this memo to do?* Then start the timer.

Sounds hokey? Hey, this hokey trick works.

When I'm up against a deadline for writing a book and find myself poking along, I set hourly deadlines. I start a timer and force myself to work against the clock for an hour at a time. You can't even guess at how this trick pumps up the productivity. You'd have to try it to believe it.

So do try the 15-second deadline. That's only enough time to think of one thing. That one thing is always the result you want to achieve with what you're about to write. It pops to the top of your mind so you can put it into your top line.

Practice the trick right now. Think of an e-mail you've been putting off. Make that e-mail the next thing you write. Set a timer. Ask yourself, *What's my bottom line?*

Go! *One-thousand-one, one-thousand-two . . .*

Dum-da-da-dee-dum. Time's up.

Got it, the one result you want out of your memo? If not, keep writing until you have identified the *what*.

Now, make that bottom line your top line and build the rest of your e-mail beneath it.

Add only as much background as you need.

If you must add references, don't copy huge amounts of boilerplate into the text block. Tell people where to go to find the references. Invite them to ask you for specific references. You'll soon find that nobody asks for the references. You'll see you've wasted a lot of effort in your writing before.

The CC Writer's Topmost Bottom Line

Think that tip was nifty? Here's an even better one:

Put your bottom line into the subject line

Did you notice that my edited samples so far did just that? In Chapter 1, the sample used the subject line:

    Subject: Salary Increase Web Forms

The revision line read:

    Subject: How to Submit Salary Increases

The first subject could refer to anything, including how to fold, spindle, and mutilate salary increase Web forms to bake a devil's food e-cake. The second one tells that a specific series of steps, a process, will follow in the text of the memo. In the Army memo, the subject was:

Subject: Aircraft Safety

Which might refer to the history of the Wright Brothers as well as recent crashes. The edited version told all in the subject line. A pilot could read it alone and know the bottom line.

Subject: Running landings and full-contact
autorotations prohibited UFN

Did you get the acronym UFN? In the Army and other places, it means *until further notice*. Do use the high-tech jargon and shortcuts that your readers use. If they know the terms, reading ease won't suffer. And why not?

Because they don't even read the terms like a lay reader would. They glance at the term, recognize it, place it in its context, and go on reading. On the other hand . . .

Don't burn out the eyes of the public with high-tech insider terms that read like Greek. Use insider talk only when talking to insiders.

Now let's get back to putting the bottom line into the subject line of your e-mails and other works.

Here's an e-mail subject your friend would pay attention to:

Subject: Let's do lunch today

Lunch is one of those *cha-ching* words like *salary* and *free*. Bringing us to an even better bottom line, a *free lunch*:

Subject: Let's do lunch today — my treat

Rest assured, your friend will open and read your e-mail. Here are some other . . .

Tips for writing subject lines as bottom lines:

- Be specific. Avoid broad topics, such as *Aviation Safety*. Write precise subjects, as in, *Ten lessons learned from last week's UH-1H crash, lessons that might save your life.*

- Cut the FWD:FWD:FWD subject lines from e-mails. When you see FWD in the subject line, you know you won't find much original. Many readers will not open FWDs. So, if you must send along text from other messages, write a specific subject. And in the text, add a personal note.

• Repeat the gist of the subject line in the text.

Your subject might read:

Have lunch with me today.

The text could open with: *Let's do a lunch date, please. 11:30 a.m. Fargo's Café. Our usual booth.*

I think you'll get a date with that approach, don't you? Bottom line? Focus. Cut to the chase.

Chapter summary

Focus on the bottom line and put it at the top of what you write. Cut to the chase. Say *what* you want, then tell *how* and *why*. Use the 15-second deadline tool to trick yourself into finding the bottom line. Put the bottom line into the subject line, when you can. When all else fails, focus.

2

Focus on the *You*, a single reader and his hot button

Pick a name and a face to write to. Not just to aim your writing to a person. But to aim your writing to that person's interests. You make him care about your stakes — when you make them, first and foremost, *his* stakes, *his* hot button. Remember, for him, *It's all about me*. Feed that need.

Let's talk about *You*

There's that word, *You* again. Part of a concept far more profound than its mere four words. It's a premise at the center of this book. All best-selling works, fiction and nonfiction depend on it. Every effective memo uses it.

Connect with your reader by paying attention to her needs instead of your own, and you will win her over.

How does this concept work? Let's begin with you.

The day that changed the world — and you

Do you recall where you were and how you felt September 11, 2001, when you saw the effects after terrorists flew two jet liners into the Twin Towers of the World Trade Center?

Of course you do. You can recall precise details. In turn, you were shocked, afraid, angry, and sad. Then later, when you learned that other terrorists had crashed two more airplanes into the Pentagon and a Pennsylvania field, your emotions grew raw. You felt as if they had attacked you in person.

Even if you live thousands of miles from Ground Zero, you were hurt. Your recall is so vivid, it might have been yesterday.

I refer you to the cover story of *The New York Times Magazine* (August 11, 2002), "Coincidence in an Age of Conspiracy," by Lisa Belkin. After a writing workshop in Chicago, I picked up the magazine at O'Hare to read on the flight home to Montana. This bold quote on page 46 hit me.

"The fact that personal attachment adds significance to an event is the reason we tend to react so strongly to Sept. 11. In a deep and lasting way, that tragedy feels as if it happened to us all."

I know what you're thinking: *What does a 9-11 story have to do with creative corporate writing?*

Stick with me. This is a profound concept, but we're in luck. Like all elegant concepts, you can grasp it easily. A step at a time, let's treat it like the priceless gem it is and examine its every facet, its depth, its clarity, its simplicity.

You can and often do connect to even the most remote events, even random events, right?

Why? Because . . .

Nature has wired you with this tendency to connect the dots. You see patterns and invent facts to explain them.

Steven Pinker, in his book, *How the Mind Works*, (Norton, 1997) tells how research subjects give meaning and even drama to dots colliding on a video screen.

Somebody gives you a set of facts, and you fit those facts into a story. You fill in the gaps in facts with logic, wild guesses, and other fictions — anything to make it make sense. Gossip gets its very life from this side of human nature. We get some of our best superstitions from it. For instance . . .

The story of the volcano and the virgin

Early one day Early Man, Geek, sees a frog snatch a butter-fly from the air and devour it in four dozen tiny gulps. That night he sees the moon disappearing in tiny gulps. He cries out to Early Woman, "Hey Gaak, there's a giant frog in the heavens eating the moon. Quick, let's sacrifice a dozen male virgins to appease the frog."

"A dozen?" says Gaak. "Good luck finding two."

An hour after Geek tosses a jack-o-lantern into the volcano, the moon returns.

"Hey, Gaak," says Geek, "we sure appeased that frog, eh?"

"Must be so. Moon come back. Good thing we only have eclipse every two year, eh?"

"Eclipse? What is eclipse?"

The secret to Creative Corporate Writing is in *You*

Not *you*. *You*, the single reader and his needs.

Let's return to Lisa Belkin's piece on coincidence. She tells of her own coincidence. One night she's nursing the sniffles at home. A friend calls to set her up on a last-minute blind date. She tries to beg off, but her friend pleads for company on her own date. Belkin gives in, but when she gets to the movie, she finds that the original date has bailed. Her friend has called in the dreaded blind-date sub. Neither of them is impressed. Both Belkin and the sub fall asleep at the movie.

Even so, they stay in touch, and four months later the guy pops the question. Later yet, they marry.

Think about it. If she curls up on the couch instead of going out 15 years ago. If the first blind date doesn't bail. *If, if, if—* Why, she might never have found the love of her life, right? What blind, freaky, magical luck.

No doubt you have such stories in your own life, stories that thrill you by a kind of magic in the luck of the draw, the flip of the coin, the road taken. Or not taken. Freaky stories you love to fire back when somebody tells you their freaky story.

So Belkin tells her freaky story to a researcher on the human mind, Ruma Falk. Falk comes back with her own tale. She is on sabbatical from Hebrew University in Jerusalem to New York. There, on a corner in Manhattan, she runs into a friend. From Jerusalem, of all things. Halfway around the world from home. What are the odds?

Each woman sees her own story as awe-inspiring.

Because, Belkin says, "The more personal the event, the more meaning we give it, which is why I am quite taken with my story of meeting my husband (because it is a pivotal moment in my life) . . . but also why Falk is not impressed at all. She likes her own story of the chance meeting on a corner better than my story, while I think her story is a yawn."

Whoa! This was my *Eureka!* I'd been looking for the key to best-selling writing. I had studied best-selling authors. I had tried strategies to write better and to teach others how to sell their work in both fiction and nonfiction. Still, I hadn't hit the jackpot. Until that moment.

To my mind, the flight came to a stop in the air over the Dakotas. This was the secret, the key to Creative Corporate Writing. This was the very secret to selling compelling fiction. All in those four power words: *Let's talk about You.*

How many times has a friend told you about a dream. What was your response? Wait, let me guess: *Oh yeah, my dream was even weirder.* As Geek might say: *Your dream boring; my dream nifty.* As in Lisa Belkin's remark: *She likes her own story better than my story, while I think her story is a yawn.*

Not to overstate the point, here is the point:

> We all see the world mainly in terms of our own interests, our own values, wants, and needs.

All the shrinks say so. Even the biggest of muck-a-mucks.

The Hierarchy of *Me*

You've heard about Abraham F. Maslow's Hierarchy of

Needs? I do take liberties with his terms in Figure 2-1, but I do so to make the point that we humans do hold ourselves in high regard. So, indulge me.

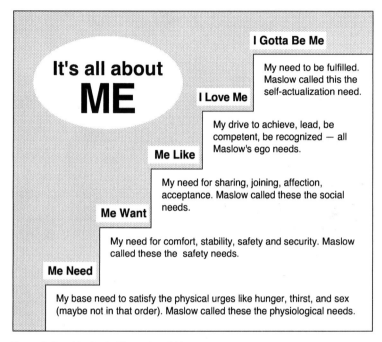

Figure 2-1 — Maslow's Hierarchy of Me.

But you don't need to go to the classics of psychology for proof. All you need to know can be found in a few moments of watching a child's behavior. Take my grandson, Dylan James Murphy, for instance, a three-year-old.

The story of ME

Not long ago, my daughter, Jill, no longer the youngster of *The Three Bears* story, thrust a camera and a dozen rolls of film at me. "Your mission is to take pictures of Dylan all day long," she said.

So Dylan and I spend the day together. I snap photos, he mugs for the camera. I stack blocks, he knocks them down. We go to the park. He wears me out.

At bedtime I win story-telling duties. I turn the events of the day into a story about Dylan. As in, "Once upon a time, a boy named Dylan lived in a house in the woods. One day his grandfather came to visit. All day long the grandfather took pictures of Dylan, read stories to Dylan ...." The story ends as Grampa "... gives Dylan a kiss, tells him good-night, turns out the light, and wishes his grandson sweet dreams."

The next night, when I go to tuck him in, Dylan does not want to hear a tale from a children's book. "Tell a story about me," he says. "Let's talk about me."

Let's talk about Me. A central need in our human nature. Most of us grow out of the urge to focus solely on ourselves. But not all of us. Some men and women never miss a chance to turn the conversation back to *Me.*

You know the type. They feed you the line, "How are you today?" You fall for it by saying, "I feel great," and they jump all over it with, "I woke up with a headache so bad it felt like I had an ax in my head." Leaving you to wish, *If only.*

On the other hand, the true masters of charisma understand how to feed that basic human need.

The Master of *Let's talk about You*

Former President Bill Clinton is a great example of *Let's talk about YOU.* Time after time, people tell stories of him entering a room and working the crowd. Clinton would go from person to person, smiling, shaking hands. He looked interested in what others had to say. He traded tidbits. He remembered the names of people he spoke to. At the end of such an event, hundreds of people would recall the night in exactly the same words: *He made me feel as if I were the only person in the room.*

My three examples: the tragedy of September 11, Dylan, and former President Clinton each show an aspect of the power of *YOU,* each in its own way.

September 11 shows how each of us can relate to a distant,

remote event to the point of personal fear, anger, and grief.

Dylan shows how we lean to our primal human nature, the *Me*, capital *M*, in each of us.

The charismatic former President Clinton shows how to play to the *Me* in others by using the *You*. Bottom line?

> The truly Creative Corporate Writer makes her writing as full of charisma on the page as Bill Clinton is in person — by using the technique of *Let's Talk about You.*

The more you can appeal to this notion, the more you make people care. And the more they care, the greater the chance your writing will compel them to action.

The bonehead who didn't read your memo? Remember him from the top of *Chapter 1*?

Next memo you write to him, work in this notion of *Let's talk about You*. Trust me, if it's about him, he'll read it. What's more, he'll remember it in detail.

But, you're asking, *What does* Let's talk about You *look like in action?*

Good question.

And the answer is: You've already seen every aspect of it in this book.

Go back to *Chapter 1*. What's the title? (*Let's talk about you*) What's the first subhead say? (*What this book can do for you*) It's all about *You*.

I use the concept of *You* all the time. I target my writing to the *You* who, if she gets what she wants, will help me get what I want. I write in the second person, to *you*, the reader.

If you're in sales, you're probably stifling a yawn of your own. You know exactly what I'm talking about. You know this concept as . . .

The hot button

To you, it's as old as old news: In any sales situation, find your prospect's hot button, then appeal to it. Put your own needs aside, and push that hot button. Forget about the features of your product, the benefits of your service. Go, go, go for the hot button and close the sale.

Congrats! You're right, as far as that thinking goes. Trouble is, it almost never goes far enough.

Think about the first sales manager who drummed the hot button into your head. He could write copy for an ad that would bring in prospects by the dozens. He'd write a pitch letter that would generate leads by the hundreds.

Then the guy would write a memo that put the staff to sleep, a report that reeked, a directive that read slow to a snail.

Why? Because he knew only to apply the hot-button concept to a clear-cut sales situation. He wasn't the truly Creative Corporate Writer who knows two crucial things about human nature and communication. First, the basic hot button for every person you write to is this:

ME — IT'S ALL ABOUT ME, ME, ME

Sorry if that tenet sounds cynical. I do believe in values and idealism. But in writing on the job, it helps to be pragmatic, too. If you want to engage a person, the best approach is, *Let's talk about YOU*. Even if you do not accept this premise as a fact of life, accept it as a central issue in CC Writing, the most basic of my 10 Suggestions on the road to being a CC Writer.

You may have been brought up in a world that talks about motivation, using the terms fear, greed, comfort, and discomfort. You know the notion: People respond only out of fear of punishment, a negative force, or to fulfill their greed. Or else they move toward comfort and away from discomfort. Forget those terms for now. *It's all about me* covers them.

Now, as to the second crucial thing that all truly CC Writers know. Namely, every human interaction is a sales situation. More to the point . . .

ALL TALK IS SALES TALK

By talk, I mean communication. The CC Writer sees a novel as sales talk, the idea of Stephen King selling his story, his talent, yes, even himself to the reader, using the concept of *Let's talk about YOU.* In other words, *If I do something for you, entertain you, scare the behemoths out of you, or thrill you with my prose, you will generate a word-of-mouth buzz about my book and buy my next novel.* So I argue . . .

- Every novel, nay, every book, is sales talk.
- Every speech is sales talk.
- Every memo is sales talk.
- Every report is sales talk.
- Every e-mail is sales talk.
- Every poem, every love letter, every prayer is sales talk, sales talk, sales talk.

You may balk at that last idea as being too cynical. Perhaps. I won't debate the issue to any length. But, arguably, even Mother Teresa had a self-interest in mind when she did her good works for the poor. In the end, she wanted to get to heaven, to be with her Creator. She said so many times.

In any case, the point of this chapter is not to debate morality and life ever after. The point is to cultivate a state of mind.

The Creative Corporate Writer state of mind

Begin with a name and a face. This frame of mind begins with the first words of this chapter. The first thing you do after you identify the bottom line result you want to achieve with your writing, is to pick your reader. Start with a person whom you identify as that single reader you want to sell to. If you're the sales manager, pick the one sales person you want to get the most response from. If you're the writer of a scientific report to be published in a journal, pick the editor you want to blow away. If you're a speaker who wants to write books to sell at the back of company meeting rooms, pick the reader you know who is sure to buy that book. Write to him. Sell to her. Find his hot button.

Bottom line, it's sales talk. Sell it to a name and a face. Two examples. Recall the memo titled:

Subject: How to submit salary increases

Clearly, it's addressed to managers who submit salary increases. If I wrote that memo, I'd have a particular person in mind, perhaps the new guy on the block, one who hasn't sent in any increases yet. Fact is, I'd ask him to proof it for me before sending it out to all other managers. Just to see if it gave him all he needed to know.

I've already talked about hot buttons, the need for managers to keep up morale by getting paychecks out on time and in the right amount. By talking to his manager and working on the draft together, I'd learn even more about his need to feed *It's all about me.*

As to the Army directive:

Subject: Running landings and full-contact
autorotations prohibited UFN

To: All 20th Aviation Division UH-1H Pilots

You may have noticed that I changed the *To:* line in my edit. The original memo went to all helicopter pilots. But the crash issue had to do only with UH-1H models. So I made it more specific. Again, the name and face I'd choose to write to would be the newest Uh-1H pilot. Her hot-button list would fill a page. On the plus-side, she'd want to look professional in a new unit. On the minus-side, she'd be afraid of breaking rules. Not to mention helicopters, her bones, and her career.

Sell to the one person only. Use this idea whether you're writing to a mass audience or to two people.

For instance, you have to write a report that will go only to the CEO and the CFO. You may be required to address your report to both, but write it to one. Yes, pick either. Put that face at the top of your mind and go to work.

Don't tell me that you have to appeal to both. If you try, you'll have about as much luck as trying to appease a spouse and a lover with a single Hallmark card. Pick one. (Or else send two cards.) It's either the CEO, who will decide, with or without the advice of the CFO. Or the CEO will defer, and the

CFO will decide. I don't know which one it will be. But you do. So, always and forever in all you write on the job . . .

WRITE TO A SINGLE PERSON

What's that you're asking?
What's the worst that can happen if I don't pick one YOU?
Answers:

❏ **You dilute the impact of your message**

Because if you write a piece for a mass audience you dilute your ability to get to *Let's talk about YOU.* You're not talking to a face in the crowd. You're talking to 10,000 faces, or ten faces. Or at least two faces. You can't get as personal when you stand on the mount and lecture to a group.

❏ **You split your personality**

Suppose you often write memos for the proles in the office. You know the boss will read it, right? So what do you do? You write it *at* the proles but *for* the boss. Admit it.

Trouble is, the instant you write for that split audience, you split your aim, your result, your appeal — and your effect.

❏ **You lose focus** on your *YOU*'s motive to act, his hot button. You lose . . . . How can I put this? Oh, I know. Remember my words from an early chapter?

> When you fail to identify a single reader to write to, you lose focus, *the* fatal flaw in today's corporate writing.

Target a single reader and you will sharpen your focus. Think. Would you rather try to push a suitcase full of hot buttons for a thousand people? Or one button for one person.

Remember, the 10 Suggestions are all about *You*. Think about the First Suggestion: Focus—make your bottom line the top line. When you cut to the chase, telling people the result you want before getting into the *why* and *how*, you are thinking of them. You are making it easy for them to see what you want. You are feeding their tendency to think: *Me, it's all about me, me, me.* You are increasing the odds that they'll put down your memo thinking: I'll say this for the writer of this piece — at least she didn't waste my time. That increases the chances they will give you what you want.

Chapter summary

Master the raw power of *Let's talk about You* in your writing and you will compel others to pay attention. The moment people see a self-interest in a piece of writing, they drop what they're doing and invest a piece of themselves in it. Don't forget, the first hot button in people's lives is to feed the notion of *Me* — *it's all about me, me, me.*

3

Focus on a single aim, either to compel or to inform

All writing is CIA writing. That is, either to Compel, to Inform, or to Amuse. Some writing serves all three aims. But the CC Writer spends a mere 15 seconds to pick a single aim to emphasize, either to compel or inform, never to amuse.

The One-Minute Creative Corporate pre-Writer

You know about the terms *compel* and *inform* already. Because we used them earlier. Let's review them in this short chapter and put our CCW pieces together. You might spend a mere 15 seconds on each of these three pre-writing tasks.

- ID your bottom line.

- Name the single reader, *You*

- Say your reader's hot button

Now take another 15 seconds to decide whether your aim is either to compel or inform. Do so and you'll be have done all the pre-writing steps to focus your Creative Corporate Writing — before you write. In only one minute.

Now, to compel? Or to inform? This ought to be clear to you before you write a word. How would you expect it to be clear to your reader if you don't have a grip on it?

It'd take you all of a second to nail this one, right? You're the boss. You want your sales staff to increase business. So you plan to publish an e-memo to raise quotas for each person. You are writing to compel higher earnings from each sales person. To do so, you will simply issue an order.

If you're the commander of that aviation unit we've been following, you want to prevent crashes in high-friction UH-1H landings. So you forbid them. You issue a written order to compel pilots to stop such landings UFN.

On the other hand, if you're a payroll division manager writing a memo to cut down salary change errors, you don't have the power to give orders to your peer managers in other divisions. But you can give clear info that will help people lower the error rate. You have critical information that will, in fact, compel those managers to go by your rules so they won't look bad to their people. Or to corporate auditors and execs.

Let's look at each of these factors.

Compelling

So far, we've used compel to issue directives or to give orders. But those terms tend to highlight the bossy aspects of compelling. The full range of meaning would include more choices:

Compel means to **Order** or to **Persuade** or to **Sell**.

You might find a dozen terms and nuances that fall between the terms I chose. I prefer not to muddy the waters. For now, use these. Then ask yourself this question:

Do I want a reader to act on my directions?

If so, your aim is to compel. Pick the term that best sets the tone you want to use. Then get to writing.

Informing

The full range of informing would include these choices:

Inform means to **Warn** or to **Advise** or to **Educate**.

Ask yourself this question:

Do I want my reader to have specific information?

If so, you've decided your aim is to inform. So pick a term that agrees with the tone you want to set.

Amusing

> Amuse? Don't do it. Not as a primary aim. The Creative Corporate Writer never writes on the job to amuse.

Trying to entertain on the job risks giving offense. One man's joke is another man's, or woman's, insult.

That's not to say you can't use your sense of humor to grab attention to support the other two functions.

Amuse means to **Dramatize** or to **Entertain** or to **Divert**.

Pick a term that supports your primary aim, either to compel or to inform. Write to compel or inform.

What if you want both to give an order and to supply the info your people need to carry out that order?

If your aim involves both, pick compel. If you give an order and tack on ten pages of info, it's an order. The order is the primary aim; the info supports the order. And don't forget to put the bottom line into the top line.

> Put the order up top. If you give a boatload of information and tack on an order, it is likely to get lost in the shuffle.

Don't we ever amuse, compel and inform at once? Yes.

For instance. A newspaper ad aims to sell eye-liner, that is, compel Janice Doe to buy the product. The ad amuses, showing a young girl applying the eye-liner to a doll. The primary aim? To compel a sale. The rest of the ad would give price, and other information that tells prospects how to buy.

Another case. The Belfry town council wants to inform citizens about a no-vote on a motion to shoo bats from city parks. Their news release uses the mildly amusing headline:

We like bats in Belfry

Okay, *really* mildly amusing. But you get the point that the primary aim is to inform, rather than to amuse.

The CCW Aiming Tool

Here are all three aims in one. The diagram speaks for itself.

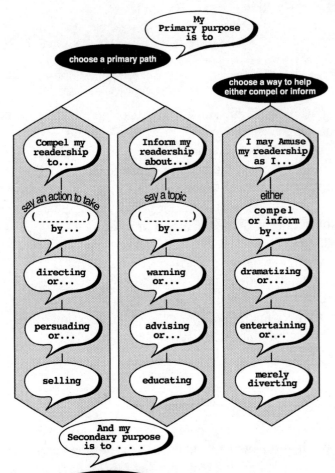

Figure 3-1 — The CC Writer Aiming Tool

Finally, before you write, focus your aim, using . . .

The One-Minute CC Writer's pre-writing job-aid

Copy this aid and carry it with you. Use it before you write.

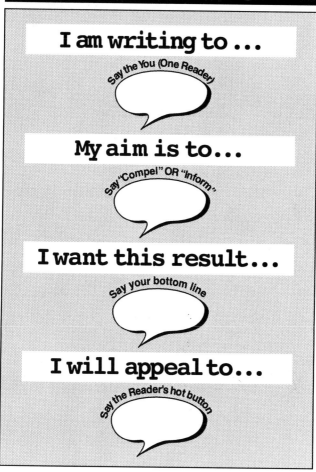

Figure 3-2 — The One-Minute CC Writer's pre-writing job-aid.

This job-aid is to get you to . . .

THINK BEFORE YOU WRITE

In a previous life, I was director of the military's journalism department at an all-services school. Long before Jay Leno's

Monday night "Headlines" segment, I would counsel military PR officers: "Read your base newspaper before your two-star general reads it."

Then I showed them why, using actual headlines I took from newspapers like the ones they would supervise. I told them about the paper at the Panama Canal's Fort Sherman, not far from the canal city of Colon.

I projected the front-page headline for the class to see:

Sergeant stabbed in Colon

Only one word for that headline: *Ouch!*

If only the writer had thought before writing it. If only the editor had stepped back with open eyes and open mind to see it on the dummy page before sending it off to the printer. If only the military PR officer had thought to check.

Odd things happen to your writing when you don't think first. So think, first to put your bottom line up top. Then to write to a single reader, the *You*, appealing to his hot button.

Chapter summary

Think before you write. Take a measly minute: 15 seconds each to pick a single aim to emphasize, either to compel or inform; 15 seconds to choose your bottom line; 15 seconds to identify your single reader, the *You*; and 15 seconds to identify your reader's hot button, you are ready to write. Remember, do not write to amuse on the job — that could get you into trouble.

4

Focus – Use the Creative Corporate Writer Reading Ease Ideal

This chapter is the heart of the book. Here you will learn how write clean text. Just write to meet or exceed my CCW Ideal. Here's the trick: If you use Microsoft Word, write no more than 15 words in your sentences. Limit words to an average of 4.5 or fewer letters. Use passive voice in no more than 2 percent of your writing. Shoot for both 75 percent readability or higher and a max level of 6 on the reading ease scales. In Corel WordPerfect's Grammatik, use the same Ideal for sentence length and passive voice, plus a max of 1.5 syllables per word, a max sentence complexity of 30 and a max word complexity of 15. **Note**: If you buy the CC Writer Ideal, and know how to use the reading ease scans, skim ahead to Chapter 5 and begin learning to edit like a pro, if you like.

Reading ease, the secret to CC Writing

I wrote and edited this book using the CC Writer Ideal, a tool that helps you read with ease. You can use the same simple tool to judge your own writing for clarity. Use it as a guide to edit your work from now on. It will help you learn to simplify, to clarify, to focus. Use it for the *YOU* in your life.

Good writing is no accident. With exception of true genius, good writers are made, not born. Teachers and coaches mold natural writing talent. With the CC Writer Ideal as your map, you can become a truly Creative Corporate Writer.

With this tool you could double or triple your ability to write clear, concise messages on the job.

Just read this chapter and apply the CC Writer Standard for Reading Ease to the next thing you write. Merely by writing with the Ideal in mind, you'll see a leap in the power of your writing. Finally, edit your work until you meet or exceed each goal in the Ideal. You'll see a second, quantum leap in the power of your writing.

Here's a chart listing . . .

The Ideals for both MS Word and Corel WordPerfect

The CC Writer's Reading Ease Ideal

Microsoft Word (Using Readability Check)

Words per sentence (avg):	15 maximum
Characters per word (avg):	4.5 maximum
Passive voice:	2% maximum
Flesch Reading Ease:	75% minimum
Flesch-Kincaid Level:	4-6

Corel WordPerfect (Using Grammatik)

Words per sentence (avg):	15 maximum
Syllables per word (avg):	1.5 maximum
Passive voice:	2% maximum
Sentence complexity:	30 maximum
Vocabulary complexity:	15 maximum

Figure 4-1 — The Creative Corporate Writer's Reading Ease ideal using Microsoft Word and Corel WordPerfect.

That's all there is to it. Five simple goals you can now use to set standards for your own writing. Five factors to use in editing your writing to a high polish. But what do they mean?

Here's the quick and dirty version, in keeping with my notion of putting the bottom line up top, I'll briefly tell you what each goal is and what to do with it. Later, I'll explain the whys and hows.

Remember. This first Ideal applies to those who use Microsoft Word, which analyzes readability with statistics a bit different from Corel's WordPerfect. No matter which word processor you use, read this discussion to get a grasp of the principles. I'll show WP users how to use the same principles with the tools of the Corel program as well.

The five goals of the CC Writer's Reading Ease Ideal—MS Word

- **Average number of words per sentence**. Shoot for an average of 15 words or fewer to increase reading ease. Readers digest short sentences best.

- **Average number of characters**, that is, letters of the alphabet, per word. Your writing should average 4.5. Short words boost reading ease like no other factor.

- **Passive voice**. This is one of only a few grammar terms you need. I'll define it later. For now, know to limit your use of the passive to 2 percent or less.

- **Flesch Reading Ease**. This is the first of two scales you can find in MS Word to test reading ease in your writing. This scale runs from 0 percent to 100 percent. The higher the percent, the better the reading ease. Strive for 75 percent or higher.

- **Flesch-Kincaid Grade Level**. This scale measures reading ease as a number from 1 to 12. As a rule, the lower the grade level in a piece of writing, the better the reading ease. In MS Word, use the ideal of four to six. Or even lower.

That's it for Word. Next let's look at . . .

The five goals of the CC Writer's Reading Ease Ideal—Corel WP

- **Average number of words per sentence**. Same as Word. Shoot for an average of 15 words or fewer.

- **Average number of syllables per word**. This is just another way of measuring word length. Your writing should average 1.5 syllables or fewer to achieve the ideal reading ease.

- **Passive voice**. Same as in Word. Limit your use of the passive voice to 2 percent or less in all your writing.

- **Sentence complexity**. WP measures sentence complexity on a scale of 0 to 100. Never exceed 30, no matter how technical your writing on the job. When you can, aim lower.

- **Vocabulary complexity** measures word length and numbers of syllables. For ideal reading ease, strive for a score of 15 or less on this 0-100 scale.

Wondering about the Flesch-Kincaid scale in WP? I don't use it. A piece of writing checked in Word rates up to two levels higher in WP. No big deal. The sentence complexity and vocabulary complexity scales are way cooler anyhow.

No matter which word processor you use, your intuition is trying to tell you there's something wrong with these goals, right? Too easy? Too direct? Relax. Look at the logic at work.

The CC Writer's Reading Ease Ideal in action

Take the memos about salary from *Chapter i*. I checked reading ease both in Word and WordPerfect. You'll want to study these results. We'll discuss how to set up your program to crunch these reading ease stats a bit later. For now, let's just look at reading ease results in both Word and WP.

Before-edit Salary Memo

Before we look at the reading ease stats on the next page, here are some overall numbers: 174 words in the body of the text, 765 characters, two paragraphs, and five sentences.

Reading Ease: Salary Memo – Before

Microsoft Word	Reading Ease	CCW Ideal
Words per sentence (avg):	34.8	15 maximum
Characters per word (avg):	4.3	4.5 maximum
Passive voice:	20 %	2% maximum
Flesch Reading Ease:	47 %	75% minimum
Flesch-Kincaid Level:	12	4-6 or lower

Corel WordPerfect	Reading Ease	CCW Ideal
Words per sentence (avg):	34.8	15 maximum
Syllables per word (avg):	1.59	1.5 maximum
Passive voice:	13 %	2% maximum
Sentence complexity:	85	30 maximum
Vocabulary complexity:	23	15 maximum

Figure 4-2 — Reading ease stats of salary memo before editing.

And here are the reading ease stats after my edit.

Reading Ease: Salary Memo – After Editing

Microsoft Word	Reading Ease	CCW Ideal
Words per sentence (avg):	11.8	15 maximum
Characters per word (avg):	3.7	4.5 maximum
Passive voice:	0 %	2% maximum
Flesch Reading Ease:	92 %	75% minimum
Flesch-Kincaid Level:	3.3	4-6 or lower

Corel WordPerfect	Reading Ease	CCW Ideal
Words per sentence (avg):	11.8	15 maximum
Syllables per word (avg):	1.29	1.5 maximum
Passive voice:	0 %	2% maximum
Sentence complexity:	14	30 maximum
Vocabulary complexity:	4	15 maximum

Figure 4-3 — Reading ease of salary memo after a CC Writer edit.

Let's study what happened here with all these factors.

Word count. I cut the piece from 174 words to 118, or 32 percent. Shorter is usually better, if you don't sacrifice clarity. As a rule, in a brief piece it's easier to find the bottom line. If a reader spends less time reading, reading ease goes up.

Characters. Again, this refers to the number of letters, numbers, and spaces (periods and commas, too) in a piece. The edit removed 302 characters, paring down the piece from 765 to 461. At a glance, this stat means nothing to you. Except. Just as a teaching point, note that the literal savings of spaces is 40 percent. The reader of the edited memo reads 40 percent fewer typing strokes, and the typist types less, too.

Paragraphs. You'll see an increase, from two to five in the body. Not a factor in reading ease statistics. But chopping a piece into more grafs makes writing easier to read. Also, the less dense a piece of writing, the more inviting it is.

Sentences. The edit doubled the number from five to 10. How this affects a piece shows up later, in the averages.

Sentences per Paragraph. For CC Writer purposes, not a factor. Too often, a run-of-the-mill corporate writer writes a single paragraph with one sentence of 50 to 100 words.

While truly Creative Corporate Writers sometimes use only one 15-word sentence in a graf.

As you can see, the number of sentences in a graf doesn't mean much to reading ease stats.

Words per Sentence. A huge factor in reading ease. I cut the average from 35 to 12, about one-third the size. That cut pumped up reading ease from 65 percent to 88 percent. Remember this fact. As a rule . . .

Simplicity rules. And nothing creates simplicity like brevity. The shorter a sentence, the higher the reading ease.

When I taught basic reporting to military students at the Department of Defense, I came across a scale that measured newspaper reader comprehension. Because it had such an effect on me, I recall it so clearly I can draw it from memory.

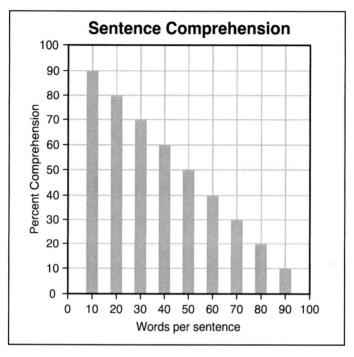

Figure 4-4 — Reading comprehension in terms of words per sentence.

From this tool I developed a 10-second tool to checking reading ease. Here's how it works:

- This sentence earned 95 percent. While this sentence, less readable, ran to 91 percent.

- Get it? (98 percent)

- Wow! (99 percent)

Look how simple that is. You count the words in a sentence and subtract from 100. That gives you a rule of thumb for gauging reading ease. A sentence with 10 words gives you 90 percent. One of 90 words, 10 percent.

Hold the figure at arm's length. Notice the straight line formed by the ends of the bars. Such a straight line means the length of a sentence has a direct, though inverse, effect on reading ease. Which means, the higher the number of words, the lower the comprehension. You don't often find correlations as direct as this outside math theory.

At this point in my workshops, some guy with a math degree asks, "Does that graph mean that if you write a memo with no words, it will have 100 percent comprehension?"

Sigh. Very funny. No. This tool does not try to say you should write zero- or one- to two-word sentences on the job.

I'm just giving you a tool that you will never forget. Every time you write a sentence, call up the mental picture of Figure 4.4. Then recall what it means. Namely, as a . . .

> Rule of thumb, if a sentence goes to 25 words, you can bet that your reader will comprehend 75 percent of it. If you write 50-word sentences—all other things being equal — expect readers to get only half of what you write. If you dare to write 75-word strings of words, well, you can do the math on that one for yourself.

Moving on.

Characters per word (MS Word). The original piece fell below the CC Writer Ideal of 4.5. My edit cut this figure from 4.3 to 3.8. A mere 12 percent gain might not strike you as much. I argue it's a major factor. But let's give the writer credit for beating the Ideal. We'll save this issue for later in the Army memo, where it shows up to a whopping degree.

Syllables per word (Corel WP). The original memo came in close to the Ideal of 1.5. The edit cut that to 1.29. Again, that's a lot more than you think, 18 percent.

Passive sentences. In the original memo's sentences, MS Word reported that the writer used passive voice 20 percent of the time; Corel WP gave us 13 percent. Don't worry about the discrepancy. Like the rest of us, not all programs see things the same way. Just chalk it up to life in the e-world. I avoid passive voice when I can, as a point of pride. I also—

What's that? You want to know: *What is passive voice?*

Good question. Let's deal with it now.

Time out to check out passive voice

Sorry to say, it's a grammar term. We can't avoid the passive voice — it affects writing power so much. So let's dig in.

On the up-side, the terms active and passive mean just what they say. In the active-voice, the subject of the sentence is an actor who acts as the verb, or action word, says to act.

On the down-side, once you get into one grammar term, other grammar terms butt in to try to help you explain the first term. Bear with me, though, and we'll get through this.

Remember the dreaded diagram from school?

Subject | verb | object

In this simple diagram of the active voice, the subject of the sentence goes ahead of the verb, or action word. The object of the sentence receives the action.

But let's get away from abstract terms. Here's an actual sentence, ripped from the headlines, in the active voice:

Rhonda eats the spider.

The subject of the sentence, *Rhonda*, acts, that is, she's the *eater*. The verb is *eats*. Not just to throw around grammar terms, but *spider* is the object, the direct object of the action acted out by the actor. Or if you like the spider is the *eatee*. Diagram it, and you get . . .

Rhonda | eats | spider

To put this crime against nature into the passive voice is simple. The subject of the sentence is acted upon. As in . . .

The spider is eaten by Rhonda.

What happened here?

Rhonda is still the *eater*. *Is eaten* becomes the action, a change from the simpler *eats*. *Spider* is still the *eatee*.

But since the *eatee* now goes before the verb, and the *eater* goes after, this is the passive voice.

Is passive voice a bad thing? No. Of course not. Let's put a reality on the table: Using passive voice is not a crime. The passive sentence is a perfectly legit writing tool. But the passive does have its down-side, too.

Let's talk about some of the ruts in the passive road.

The pitfalls of passive voice

Passive voice uses more words than active voice to express the same idea. *Rhonda eats the spider* grew from four words to six. Big deal, you say.

In fact, it is a big deal. That's a 50 percent increase in the number of words — in one sentence. If you agree with a central tenet of my logic so far in this book, reading ease suffers the more words you use. What's more . . .

Passive voice softens the impact of writing. Is that a bad thing? Perhaps not, in fiction and diplomacy. But it is when you want to cut to the chase in your writing. Take a slice from our salary memo:

```
. . . we are requesting that all salary
increase forms be submitted to the SALVO
box . . .
```

Be submitted is a passive verb that needs extra words to both prop it up and tone it down. To say the same thing in the active voice, you are free to write to the point:

```
Submit your salary increase forms to the SALVO
box.
```

Passive voice is often vague, dodging responsibility — or more often, blame. For instance, you don't get your paycheck one Friday. You call a payroll clerk to complain. She tells you, "Your paycheck was lost."

You say, "Now hold on here. I want to know who's responsible for losing my paycheck."

And she says, "Too bad, I just used the passive voice and I don't have to say."

Strictly speaking, she's right. Her first sentence dodges responsibility, all too common in corporate writing.

Contrast that with a phone call you get later in the day.

"Good news," she says, "*I* found your paycheck."

Oh, sure. Now she uses the active voice. And why, class? Of course, she wanted no part of the loss, but now she wants full credit for the find. See how that works?

When you can, take a stand. Use the active voice.

Passive voice is harder to read and understand. And not

just because it uses more words. In long sentences, you often have to re-read parts of it to find the bottom line or to search for the actor, if one even exists, because it's at the tail end.

So. That's the passive. Get it? Good. Now, here's the cool thing about this issue of passive voice. You don't have to remember it. Because high-end programs like Microsoft Word and WordPerfect will check your writing for passive voice and give you a report.

A quick review of passive voice and a brief quiz

When the subject of a sentence, the word before the verb or action word, acts, that's active voice. When the subject is acted upon, that's passive voice.

Final test — active or passive?

The spider ate Rhonda.

Don't blurt. Think *eater* and *eatee* and their positions in the sentence before you answer. Re-read the quick review.

Now, which is it?

You say active? Great. You're right.

Now let's get back to . . .

Reading Ease Ideals, continued

The readability scales. These are programs built into your high-end word processor, Word or WP, to measure reading ease.

Most of them compare the number of syllables to the number of words and average number of words in a sentence and multiply by a secret, small number with lots of digits behind the decimal point to get to their scale. The precise details of the process don't matter as much as how the scales report their results.

Flesch Reading Ease (MS Word). On this scale of 0 to 100 percent, the higher the number, the higher the reading ease. In our original salary memo, we see readability of 47 percent. A simple edit raised that score to 92 percent, well above the CC Writer Ideal of 75 percent.

Flesch-Kincaid Reading Ease in Word. This scale reports a grade level as its result of checking your writing. The scale reported that the original memo scored at the 12th grade. The revision scored 3.3. Flesch and Kincaid tell us that if a sample rates a score at the eighth-grade level, the average American eighth-grader will grasp what you wrote.

Get all that business about grade levels? Good, now forget it. Just use the numbers I gave you, a max of 6 in MS Word.

> Forget the term, grade levels, in Flesch-Kincaid. For me, they have nothing to do with grade levels in school. It's just a number I use to set a goal for you to aim for.

So don't try to write like a fifth-grader or to a fifth-grade kid. I didn't edit the memo by dumbing down to third-graders. I just wrote it to meet the 75 percent ideal on one scale and the 4-6 ideal on the other. Grade level doesn't mean a thing.

For one thing, who knows what an average fourth-grader can read? Some of them can read software code. Others still don't get *Goldilocks and The Three Bears*.

For another thing, if you have a recent version of Word, Flesch-Kincaid only goes up to grade 12. I guess the creators of the scale or writers of the software program found too much bad writing out there. The scale used to report reading ease levels at grade levels past 16. That doesn't mean much in the real world.

Just for the heck of it, though, I tested the "Before" salary memo on an older computer with an earlier version of Word and found that the memo tested at the 15th grade. The Army memo went all the way to the 17th grade.

I wish they'd left the program alone. I have put the test to some corporate writing and found numbers that went past 20th grade. You lose the effect of how bad a piece of writing can be when it tops out at the ceiling of 12. In WordPerfect the scale tops out at the 16th grade, again, whatever that is.

You'll remember I said to ignore the Flesch-Kincaid scale in WordPerfect. That's because WP checks writing on two other scales that give you far better control.

Sentence Complexity Scale. Look here. This sentence is simple. It rated 1 percent on the Corel WP scale. Long sentences, with phrases between commas, or joined by semicolons or conjunctions like *but, or,* and *and,* are harder to read and rate higher on the scale; for instance, this sentence rated 50 percent, with a 43 percent vocabulary complexity besides. See how that works? The "Before" salary memo scored 85 out of 100. That's macro-ugly. Writing like that is hard to follow. After the edit, the memo rated a 14, well within the Ideal standard of 30. Best of all, you found it far easier to read.

Vocabulary Complexity Scale. This scale measures the ill effect of complex words on reading ease. The "Before" memo rated 23. The edit took the score down to 4. Well under the Ideal max of 15.

To get the maximum out of reading ease scales, meet all five standards for the word processing program you use.

Using the CC Writer Ideal on the job

Rocket science it ain't. Follow these steps.

- **Write a first draft** of your piece, memo, letter, directive, report, analysis, whatever.

- **Analyze your piece** using the grammar tool or combination spell-check-grammar-check tool in MS Word or Grammatik in Corel WordPerfect.

- **Check the results** against the CC Writer Reading Ease Ideal for your word program.

- **Revise and edit** your piece until it meets each goal in the Ideal.

Let's look at each of these steps in greater detail.

Write your piece

Simple enough. Just do it, as the Nike ads used to say. Now that you've read this far in the chapter, you'll probably write with several notions in mind. These, for instance:

- Focus—make your bottom line the top line.

- Focus on the *You*, a single reader.

- Focus on a single aim, to compel or to inform.

- Focus on writing short sentences, small words, and in the active voice.

Check the results against the CC Writer Reading Ease Ideal

Select the text you want to analyze. You need to know two things about the extremes of selecting either a tiny amount of text or a mountain of text.

Thing One: Checking small amounts of text. If you select only two words in a sentence to check reading ease — and why you would is beyond me — the program will check the entire sentence. If you really only want to check two words, highlight them, copy them into a new document, add a period, and run the check.

Thing Two: Checking large amounts of text. If you wish to check a long report or even a book, don't run the entire document at once. For two good reasons:

- It can take forever to get stats in a long document in Word.

- The scan will average out the easy-to-read parts of the book with the complex parts. You may get a result that meets the ideal overall, but find that some segments are pure Greek.

Rule of thumb. Run your scans on fewer than five pages at a time. If you can, run a scan on pages that cover a single topic. Then edit a segment at a time.

NOTE: You can set your computer to scan text *or* skip this stuff

WordPerfect users, skip to page 66. If you know how to get readability stats, skip to page 70: *Scanning your own work.*

Setting up MS Word to get Reading Ease stats

With your file open . . .

1. Open the *Tools* menu in Word and select *Preferences*. Click the *Spelling & Grammar* tab in the dialogue box.

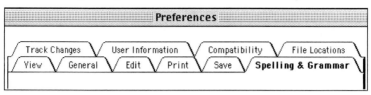

Figure 4-5 — Tabs you'll see after selecting Preferences.

2. Set choices in *Spelling & Grammar*. I check the boxes on my Mac, just as you see them in Figure 4-6.

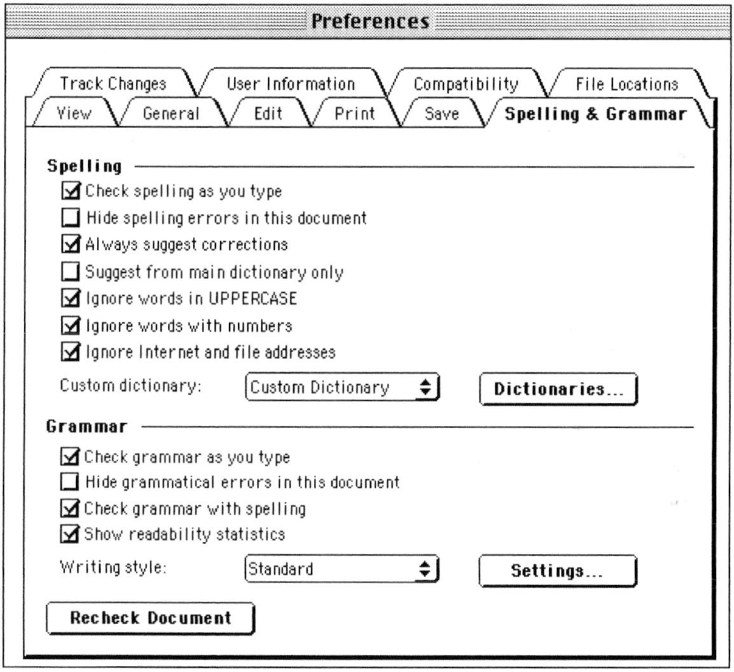

Figure 4-6— Boxes to check under Spelling & Grammar preferences.

I recommend checking these three at least:

Ignore words in UPPERCASE

Ignore words with numbers

Ignore Internet and file addresses

That way your company acronyms and long strings of words and numbers won't lower your reading ease scores.

As to the box labeled *Writing style*: I select *Standard*. Far as

I know, the other choices won't affect reading ease scores.

3. Check the box labeled: *Show readability statistics* under *Spelling & Grammar*. You *MUST* check this box to get stats for the Creative Corporate Writer Ideal.

4. Select the *Settings* button.

Under *Grammar and style* options, as in Figure 4-7, check as few boxes as you can live with. The more boxes you check, the longer it takes to run reading ease scans.

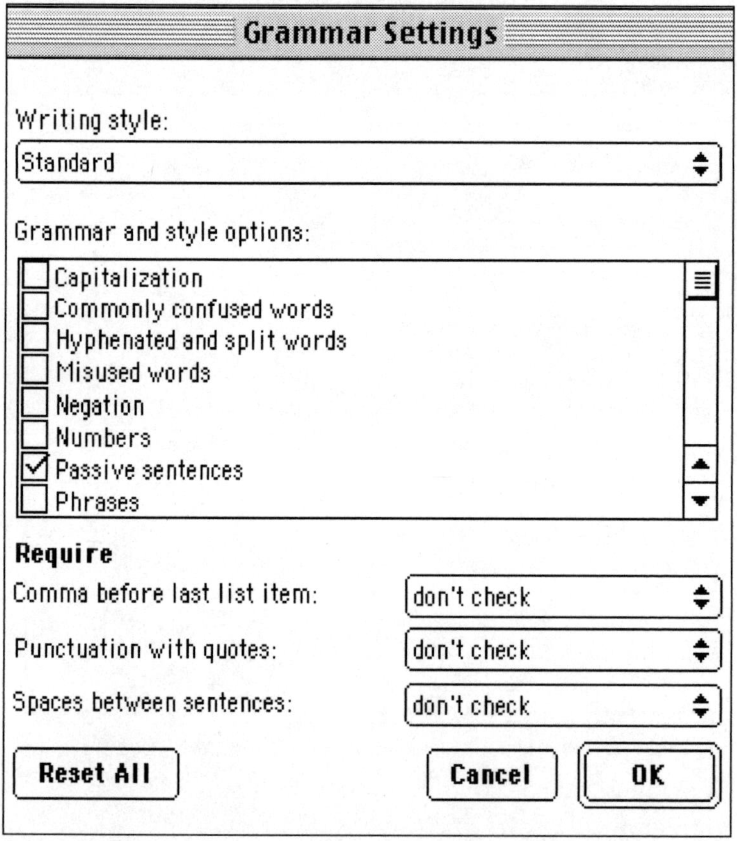

Figure 4-7 — Grammar and style options and the Require choices.

5. You *MUST* check the box titled *Passive sentences*. It's one of the factors in the CC Writer Ideal, after all.

Scroll down in this segment of the box to see other options like these:

Grammar and style options:

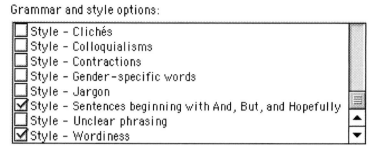

Figure 4-8 — More Grammar and style options.

I always ask Word to call my attention to *Sentences beginning with And, But,* and *Hopefully*. I seldom use *Hopefully* in any context. But all too often, I fall victim to the tendency to lead off with the other two offenders. And this option keeps me on my toes most of the time. But not all of the time.

6. Under *Style* select *Wordiness*. This option points out long sentences during the grammar check. It's a help to you in the edit process. I use it, but you don't need it for stats.

7. Under *Require*, I suggest you choose *don't check* as your option under each of the categories there. It simply saves time as the computer analyzes your work.

8. Click *OK* buttons until you get back to your document.

Now you're ready to go. Under the *Tools* menu, select *Grammar*. If you don't select any text before this step, the program will check the entire file and bring up your stats. If you have selected only part of the file to check, remember to choose *No* when Word offers to check the rest of the document, as in this message:

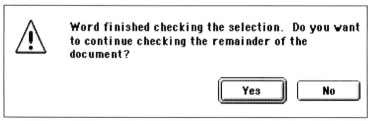

Figure 4-9 — Choose NO in this box to get readability stats in Word.

This brings up the box titled *Readability Statistics*, giving you the stats you need to check your reading ease against the CC Writer's Ideal.

```
═══════════════ Readability Statistics ═══════════════

Counts
    Words                                          174
    Characters                                     765
    Paragraphs                                       2
    Sentences                                        5
Averages
    Sentences per Paragraph                        2.5
    Words per Sentence                            34.8
    Characters per Word                            4.3
Readability
    Passive Sentences                              20%
    Flesch Reading Ease                           47.0
    Flesch-Kincaid Grade Level                    12.0

                                          ┌─────────┐
                                          │   OK    │
                                          └─────────┘
```

Figure 4-10 — Readability stats in Word for the "Before" salary memo.

Before you close that box, capture the stats. Better yet, let the computer do it for you.

How to take a picture of the screen with the stats on it

This depends on whether you have a Mac or PC. Either way, it's easy to do.

On the Mac

With your Mac's *Finder* window active, hold down both the *shift key* and *command (Apple)* key and hit the *?* key.

That brings up a help window. In the blank space, type the words, *screen picture*, then click the *Search* button.

That will bring up index entries to get you where you want to go. In older versions, select the line that reads: *Take a "snapshot" of the screen?* to highlight it.

Then click on the *OK* button, which will take you to the page that tells you how to capture a screen.

With my operating system, version, 9.1, I get a choice from three sets of keystrokes. Like this . . .

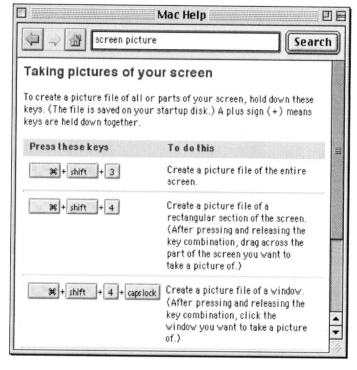

Figure 4-11 — Mac System 9.1 options for capturing data on screen.

I use the *Shift+Command+4* combination because I can outline a portion of the text as well as the stats. At a glance I can see which version of the text the stats apply to.

Oh, and you need to know this: Your Mac saves your first image to your hard drive with the label *Picture 1*. The next image after is called *Picture 2*, and so on.

To open one of these pictures double-click on it and print once it's open. Or print it just by selecting it and typing *Command+P*. Here's another tip:

If you work with lots of printouts, label your hard copies of pictures and give your picture files matching names. Otherwise, you'll forget what image is in each file and have to open them all to go on hunts. Hey, been there, done that.

Saving pictures on a PC using Windows

You can take a picture of the entire screen and all that's showing just by pressing the key labeled *Print Screen*.

Or, you may just want the stats. With your readability stats showing and the word file as the active (selected) window, hold down the *ALT* key and press that *Print Screen* key again.

The picture will print. It's also in memory. You can open a new word processing document and paste several image into it using the command *Control+V*. Print the page and label it for your records.

> Keep copies of the reading ease stats for your "Before" documents so you can track the progress of your edits.

And there you have it. Trust me, this is way simpler than my explanation of it. In any case, once you set the preferences, it's done forever, or at least until the next time you want to change them.

Getting Reading Ease stats in Corel WordPerfect

This is almost too simple. First because you don't need to either go through an elaborate setup or run a full spelling or grammar check to get stats. Second because the program runs those reading ease stats in an instant.

1. Open the *Tools* menu and select *Grammatik* in the document that you want to check for reading ease.

2. Select *Options* from among the offerings that appear.

3. Select *Analysis* from the new choices offered.

4. Select *Readability* from the final choices, which gives you the window on the next page with almost no waiting.

Some of what you see may be new to you, so let's discuss WordPerfect reading ease features that haven't yet come up.

Comparison document. You see the words, *Hemingway*

short story, in the slot. WP compares your tested file to several choices in the program. The short story, the Gettysburg Address, and IRS instructions for the form 1040EZ. Hemingway comes up each time your run Grammatik. I say ignore Hemingway. You're comparing your work to the CC Writer Ideal now. In fact, I added the CC Writer Ideal to Figure 4-12 so you could compare results to it.

Reading Ease in WP: Salary Memo After Editing

Comparison document. Hemingway short story ▼   Add Document...

Flesch-Kincaid grade level*

Salary memo after	4.43	*Ignore Flesch-Kincaid
Hemingway	4	in Corel Word Perfect

Passive voice (% of finite verb phrases)

Salary memo after	0
Hemingway	3
CC Writer Ideal	2 percent maximum

Sentence complexity (100 = very complex)

Salary memo after	14
Hemingway	14
CC Writer Ideal	30 maximum

Vocabulary complexity (100 = very complex)

Salary memo after	4
Hemingway	5
CC Writer Ideal	15 maximum

Flagged...   Basic Counts...   Close   Help

Figure 4-12 — WordPerfect reading ease, salary memo after editing.

If you want to add a document of your own and use it as the standard, fine. Just run the stats check on a piece of your work that meets the CC Writer Ideal. Then click on the button . . .

Add Document. From now on, your work will be there as one of the choices for WP to use for comparison. When you check reading ease in WP, the Hemingway stats will pop up because, as I say, it's the default scale. To get to your standard, click on the words, *Hemingway short story*, and highlight the name of your own scale when it appears with the others. Grammatik will reset the bars and scales to the new standard so you can compare yourself to yourself. Cool, huh?

Flesch-Kincaid grade level. I've already said to ignore this scale in WordPerfect. If you insist on using it, try an ideal level of 8 for starters. Work down as you get better at editing.

Passive voice. This we've discussed. You see that Hemingway goes beyond the CC Writer Ideal. But his sample is fiction, after all. You see that he falls inside the fiction writer's max of 5 percent. You see that is good.

Sentence and Vocab complexities. Enough said already.

Basic Counts. Click this button to get the rest of your stats. You'll get a window that looks like Figure 4-13.Once again, I drew in the CC Writer Ideal so you could compare results.

Basic Counts: Salary Memo After Editing

COUNTS:

Syllables	155	Short sentences	5
Words	120	Long sentences	0
Sentences	0	Simple sentences	7
Paragraphs	6	Big words	5

AVERAGES:		**CC Writer Ideal**
Syllables per word	1.29	1.5 maximum
Words per sentence	12	15 maximum
Sentences per paragraph	1.66	

Figure 4-13 — WordPerfect basic counts, "After" salary memo.

Note *Averages*, which we've discussed to death. Also *Big words*. In WP, if it has more than six letters, it's a big word.

Flagged. If you choose this button, WP will give you a list of grammar issues that the program sees as possible problems. In the "After" salary memo, here's what you see:

Flagged Window: Salary Memo After Editing

Below are the rules flagged in your document. A flagged rule represents a potential error.

FLAGS	RULE CLASS
3	Second-Person Address
3	Spelling
1	Paragraph Problem
1	Wordy

Total potential errors flagged in document:	8

Figure 4-14 — Flagged issues in "After" salary memo in Corel WP.

I don't use this tool. As you already know, I use *you*, the second-person address, as much as I can in my writing. It's a way to keep my writing informal and personal. It's no error. Rather, it's an integral part of the Creative Corporate Writer system.

The *Spelling* flags refer to acronyms the spell-check found.

I deal with the other issues using the Creative Corporate Writer Ideal. But use the grammar check if it helps you.

Just for the record, I'll share some reading ease stats from the text of this book.

Look to the next page for the figures for *Chapter i, Let's talk about you.*

To be fair to me, I deleted the bad example, "Salary Increase Web Forms," before running the reading ease check. And no, I didn't write the chapter to final draft quality on my first try. Using the Ideal as a guide, I revised and edited to a high polish to get to the final stats in Figure 4-15. I kept at it until I met or bested every item in the Ideal. Take a look.

Reading Ease Results of Chapter i of this Book

Microsoft Word	Reading Ease	CCW Ideal
Words per sentence (avg):	10.6	15 maximum
Characters per word (avg):	4.3	4.5 maximum
Passive voice:	0 %	2% maximum
Flesch Reading Ease:	79.7 %	75% minimum
Flesch-Kincaid Level:	4.7	4-6 or lower

Corel WordPerfect	Reading Ease	CCW Ideal
Words per sentence (avg):	10.58	15 maximum
Syllables per word (avg):	1.43	1.5 maximum
Passive voice:	0 %	2% maximum
Sentence complexity:	14	30 maximum
Vocabulary complexity:	11	15 maximum

Figure 4-15 — Chapter i reading ease in both programs.

I'm happy with the result. I think I could lower the numbers in every category but passive voice, in every chapter. But showing off is not the point. Reading ease is the point. Reading ease by meeting the Creative Corporate Writer's Reading Ease Ideal. Now, why don't you just try . . .

Scanning your own work

For the first time in your writing life, you have a guide to use in writing, in editing, and in checking the work of others. It's the Creative Corporate Writer's Ideal.

To get a true sense for the value of this CC Writer Ideal, you need to use it on a typical piece of corporate writing. Say from a Web page of any Fortune 500 company. Or even your own firm. Maybe even your own writing.

Pick a company, any company. Go to the Web site. Select a

page or two of text, copy it, paste it into a word processing file, remove the extra line returns, and run the scan.

I've done dozens.

Every time I do a workshop, I visit the Web sites of my client. I test e-mails, letters, memos, and other pieces of writing, often in the *About Us* link. I also look into the Web pages of other major firms in the same region.

What do I find? Without fail, the material flies off the charts in reading ease. Or should I say reading difficulty?

Even on pages aimed at an average reader, I find stuff written at only 15 percent comprehension on the Flesch scale and 17th grade on the Flesch-Kincaid. Sentence complexity is a jungle, with 60-plus words in them. Average character-per-word length goes to 8 in Word and complexity scores go to 50+ in WP. Passive voice reeks at 40 percent or higher.

Even in companies where you'd expect to find good writing. Brief example. I often go to the online page of a major daily paper and check the reading ease of the day's news stories. Most often they meet the Ideal. Even technical news stories don't go far past the CC Writer Ideal. That's because these writers learn in J-school to avoid the passive, to write short sentences, and so on. Some fall into bad habits, but the best writers keep to a high ideal of their own.

Then I go to *About Us* on the site. You'd think with all the writers and editors on staff that a newspaper would use that talent in writing to the public. Nope. Many papers sling garbage onto the Web pages and forget it.

My overall conclusion? Corporate writing is in a sorry state. It's flabby as a pig's jowls and twice as dense, mate, just the kind of writing your readers love to hate.

That's the down-side.

The up-side?

You can use the Ideal to edit your writing until it sparkles

You can easily fix flabby writing. Anybody with a set of standards and a modest amount of talent can cut the flab.

I've given you the standard so you can first identify the flab.

You now have an ideal to write to. All you need now is a process for editing.

Which is where we're going next. The remaining chapters in this book will tell you the steps to cut a given piece of writing down to the CC Writer Ideal or to boost reading ease.

I'll shut the page on this chapter with these thoughts:

> Writing is wa-a-ay over-rated. You show me a Creative Corporate Writer, and I'll show you somebody who knows how to edit her own work using the CC Writer Reading Ease Ideal.

How do most writers handle a routine e-memo? They knock it out and maybe, *maybe*, run a spell-check before firing it off.

Why are they so hasty? Are they bad people? Heck no. Once they finish writing, they don't know what else to do. Be honest. You've gazed at a piece of your own writing until your eyes glazed over, wondering, wondering. *Is this good enough?* you wonder. *What needs fixing?* you ask yourself. Truly rhetorical questions they are, too.

> In the past, you didn't know where to begin editing or what standards to apply to an edit. Until now. Now you have the CCW Reading Ease Ideal. Now you have a road map.

In fact, the truly Creative Corporate Writer has both a road map and a destination. He runs the Reading Ease Scan. Then he revises and edits. He checks the reading ease stats again. Edits. Scans. Revises. Scans. Edits. Until he brings in an e-memo that meets or exceeds each goal in the Ideal. Then and only then does he tap the *Send* button.

In the next three chapters, let's see how he works his magic.

Chapter summary

You can cut the flab out of your writing and the writing of others. All you need to know is where to begin and where to go. To that end I give you the CC Writer Ideal. Set up your computer and test your own writing and that of your firm. Then use the Ideal as a guide for editing.

5

Focus your edit
on writing short words

This is the biggest little writing secret Creative Corporate Writers must master. Nothing boosts reading ease more than using short words. No matter how technical your field.

A few *short* lessons

For the record, the Microsoft Word manual says you should try for a score of 60 to 70 in reading ease on the Flesch scale and seventh- to eighth-grade level on the Flesch-Kincaid Scale. Forget that. Those numbers don't cut it. Like most lessons in my life, I learned this one the hard way.

Lesson 1: Out of chaos, the discovery of the Reading Ease Ideal

I was deep into writing a book for novelists, *The Fiction Writer's Brainstormer* (Writer's Digest Books, 2000). While tossing around some crazy ideas for ways to look at how to revise and edit, I decided to study success. Success of best-selling authors. I chose my favorite author and my least favorite. I chose women and men, current novels and works out of the past. Only one thing mattered: the writers had to be best-sellers.

My findings changed my writing life forever and led directly to the concept of *The Creative Corporate Writer* and my next book, *Compelling — The Road to Best-Selling*.

I analyzed the writing of these best-selling authors: Fannie Flagg (*Fried Green Tomatoes at the Whistle Stop Cafe*), Kaye Gibbons (*Ellen Foster*), John Grisham (*The Street Lawyer*), Jan Karon (*A New Song*), Stephen King (*Misery*), Elmore Leonard ("Hanging out at the Buena Vista," a short story) Terry McMillan (*How Stella Got Her Groove Back*), Anna Quindlen (*One True Thing*), Danielle Steel (*Star*), and Wallace Stegner (*Angle of Repose*).

Why would I evaluate an escapist romantic novel by Danielle Steel next to *Angle of Repose* by Wallace Stegner, which won the Pulitzer Prize?

To be honest, I don't know why I put them side-by-side. Except that *Angle of Repose* is one of my favorite novels, and I wanted to compare it to something less favorite. I admit I'm not a fan of Danielle Steel. But I know she is popular and successful. I respect her success, and I wanted to learn how and why she earns it each time she delivers a new book.

Here's how I compared the authors. I tested samples of the novels and the entire short story of Elmore Leonard. I put the samples into Word documents and ran the reading scans. (To be objective, I took the opening 700 words or so from each novel and another 700 words or so from the very center of each book. To be subjective, I also took high-energy samples from the end of each book, dipping into the climax, where you'd expect to find the best writing.) Except for the short story, each total sample was 2,000 words or longer.

In a star-studded, but diverse, list like that, you wouldn't expect to find much in common, would you? I mean, besides their fat royalty checks, right? Wrong.

Imagine how stunned I was to see not one, but several things in common emerge, things that you and I can use.

But with my typing fingers trembling, I knew I had to double-check those findings. So I tested several control samples against the best-sellers. I used a scene from my own novel, a piece from an unpublished novelist who had sent a manuscript for me to critique, and a selection from the U.S. government. I used a Medal of Honor citation, which I thought would rank better than average government writing.

I was stunned again by this further result:

> **B**est-selling authors share several critical traits in their writing. What's more, most other writers, whether in fiction or non-fiction, do not share those traits with the best-selling authors.

What are these traits? You already know them, of course. They are the five elements of the CC Writer's Ideal.

- Short sentences
- Short words
- Active voice
- High reading ease on the Flesch scale
- A level of 6 or lower on the Flesch-Kincaid scale

Heck, that should be no surprise. I found those factors in those best-selling books and adapted them for you. Are they the same standards as those in your CC Writer Ideal? No.

Clearly, authors of best-selling novels, corporate writers, newspaper reporters, and tech writers have different audiences. One size Ideal may not fit all.

In *The Fiction Writer's Brainstormer*, I laid out my first Reading Ease Ideal for novelists.

Lesson 2: Reading Ease Ideal for novelists

- No standard for sentence length
- An average 4.25 characters a word
- Passive voice in no more than 5 percent of sentences
- A score of 80 percent or higher on the Flesch scale
- 4-6 on the Flesch-Kincaid scale

Why the difference for fiction writers?

On sentence length, I give fiction writers artistic license to vary sentence length. CC Writers need a stricter set of goals because lack of focus is such an issue in corporate writing. Even so, in my fiction, I try for an average of 12 to 15 words.

On characters per word. I hold novelists to a stricter Ideal. A corporate writer is stuck with long words. On Wall Street, for instance, writers have to live with terms like *portfolio diversification*. Two words, 25 characters, and 10 syllables.

On passive voice. Novelists get more slack, up to 5 percent, rather than the 2 percent max I gave to CC Writers. In fiction, passive voice can help a writer pace a scene by slowing action. Corporate writers needn't worry about pace. Logic, and reading ease count for so much more.

On the Flesch scale, I went to 80 percent as a minimum. I also think a novelist should write high-energy scenes in the 90+ range on Flesch and 3-4 in Flesch-Kincaid.

On my own novel. I had one of those *Eureka!* moments when I tested a book of my own. I'd already sent a *Force Recon* action novel to Penguin Putnam. I'd already tested it for reading ease, using Microsoft's standards. But the novel fell short of the new standard, which I now saw as critical. So I called my editor and got it back from production. In a most hectic week, I revised the book scene by scene, using the Ideal I'd set for novelists. The result was worth the effort.

Lesson 3: Editing that matters most

Before I went through the work of re-editing my novel, I had to know: What editing steps would have the most effect?

I edited one scene four times, each time starting with the original piece of writing because I wanted to control the test and find out which edits really mattered. Here's how it went:

- On the first edit, I changed passive voice to active only, to see what effect that would have on reading ease. I made no other changes, except to move words around to keep the sense of the writing.

- On the second edit of the original piece, I deleted words where I could and did nothing else.

• On the third edit, I cut sentences apart with periods. I made word changes only to keep the sense of the piece.

• On the fourth edit, I cut big words down to size.

By now I think you can guess which edit had the best effect on reading ease. Yep, cutting big words.

Kick the tires on this brief demo. I made one edit to that sentence from page 76 so it reads: "On Wall Street, for instance, writers have to live with terms like *PD*." Just look at the stats.

Editing Results — After Cutting Two Words

Microsoft Word	Before	After	CCW Ideal
Words per sentence (avg):	14	13	15 maximum
Characters per word (avg):	5.5	4.3	4.5 maximum
Passive voice:	0 %	0 %	2% maximum
Flesch Reading Ease:	47.5 %	96 %	75% minimum
Flesch-Kincaid Level:	10	3	4-6 or lower

Corel WordPerfect	Before	After	CCW Ideal
Words per sentence (avg):	14	13	15 maximum
Syllables per word (avg):	1.92	1.46	1.5 maximum
Passive voice:	0 %	0 %	2% maximum
Sentence complexity:	7	6	30 maximum
Vocabulary complexity:	51	10	15 maximum

Figure 5-1 - Results after editing just two words: portfolio diversification.

Don't get crazy over that result, okay. Small changes in short pieces do have a big effect. I warn you, don't run reading ease scans on each sentence. Scan the completed piece in no more than five-page chunks. Now you may have a question or two about that little demo. Hold them. We'll come back to it later, and I'll give you some answers. Now, let's get down to editing words, shall we?

How to shorten words for reading ease

The bottom line — take a stand

Stop trying to hide behind big words and the passive voice. Be honest. You think it's too raw to say what you mean. You learned the corporate jargon and you're danged well going to use it. A guy can get fired if he writes a memo that doesn't leave a bit of wiggle-room in it.

Where do these ideas come from? If the boss wants to fire you, you're toast. No matter how clever your memo wording.

To review. Cut to the chase. Write in the active voice. Say what you mean. If it helps, let me put it this way . . .

> Never trust a word with four syllables. And be wary of any word with just three. Find a shorter word, if you can.

What's that? You're worried that people won't respect you if you don't prove yourself by using bigger words?

Hey, as the character Annie Wilkes said in Stephen King's book *Misery* and the movie of the same name: "Have you got amnesia?"

I put this worry into the same category as leaving wiggle-room. You're thinking of yourself. You're not thinking of your reader, the *YOU* you should write to.

Look, I love words big and small. I've spent my life building my vocabulary. But my study of best-selling writing taught me a lesson in humility. The Pulitzer-Prize-winning author Wallace Stegner's literary novel, *Angle of Repose*, is an elegant work of art. It beat out my *Force Recon* action-novel for reading ease before I took it back for revision. I'll grant that my book beside Stegner's is still literary-lite. Nobody but an idiot would argue that *Angle of Repose* was written for a fifth-grader or with a fifth-grade vocabulary.

> It's not the size of the vocabulary you own that matters to reading ease; it's the size of the vocabulary you use.

For the last time, using big words doesn't make you superi-

or to your reader. In fact, using big words, by making your writing hard to read, has just the opposite effect. So . . .

Avoid pompous words and phrases

Use plain words. Don't *eliminate* when *cut* works as well. Don't *terminate* when you can *fire*. What are *extenuating circumstances*? Do you mean *excuses*? *Reasons*? *Problems*?

Attitudinal? *Institutionalize*? *Recapitulate*? A break, please.

As for shorter words, they can be obnoxious, too. Don't use *initiate* when *start* will do. Same with *optimum* versus *best* and *utilize* versus *use*. Be suspicious of all words that end in *-ize* or *-ization*. Use a thesaurus to find the shortest word that does the job. I prefer *The Synonym Finder* (Rodale Press).

And why write this?

> We are requesting your objective consideration
> of our recommendation.

When you can say it better with this:

> Please take a look at this suggestion and get
> back to me.

I'll tell a story on myself here. Before I discovered the Ideal, I wrote a book for Writer's Digest called *You Can Write a Novel*. One piece of advice I gave was to:

> Eliminate body language verbalizations in dia-
> logue.

What was I thinking? What I meant to say was:

> Don't let your characters spit, grin, snort,
> giggle, or grunt their lines.

Shun -tion words

Don't smother your verbs, as in:

> He requested the cooperation of the department
> but nobody accepted his recommendation for the
> adoption of the plan of attack.

When you mean to say:

> He asked his team to cooperate, but nobody
> accepted his plan.

Don't use -ly words

I'm talking adverbs here.

Adverbs rarely carry a memo authoritatively. The common corporate writer severely taxes her brain, striving earnestly to write professionally, only to find herself studiously ignored.

Let's edit the adverbs out of that graf, shall we? How is this?

```
Adverbs won't carry a memo. The common corpo-
rate writer taxes her brain, striving to write
with adverbs, only to find herself ignored.
```

Do you see how well the verbs, *carry, taxes, striving, write,* and *ignore* stand on their own? Forget about how many syllables I cut from the bad example. For the moment, forget about reading ease statistics. You (and *YOU*) see how the second version reads better? Enough said. Speakina which . . .

Don't use endless synonyms for said

Just use *said* instead of:

added	admitted	advised	affirmed	agreed
answered	argued	avowed	claimed	commented
confessed	continued	declared	emphasized	explained
observed	maintained	opined	queried	quipped
related	remarked	replied	reported	revealed

All are longer than *said.* Some add an extra sense that the writer is adding an opinion. When you write: *The CFO confessed to an error in the annual report*, it sounds as if you're saying you caught her cooking the books.

Swat the "Atomic Flyswatters"

It's Theodore M. Bernstein's term (*The Careful Writer*, Atheneum) for words a writer uses, hoping to inject dull writing with dramatic effect. Find these words and write them out of your writing:

amazing	awful	divine	dreadful	earthshaking
enormous	fabulous	fantastic	frightful	sensational
horrible	petrified	gorgeous	super	stupendous
tremendous	terrible	wonderful	awesome	unbelievable

Clean up the bureaucratese

Here's another list for you. Some of these expressions have four small words, but they can be cut to one.

Search your writing for words in the first column. When you find one, pick a replacement from the second column.

in order to	to
for the purpose of	to
in the near future	soon
in the event that	if
additional	added, more, other
afford an opportunity	allow, let
approximately	about
as a consequence	so
at the present time	now
fatuous numbskull	jerk
disseminate	issue, send out
due to the fact that	due to, since
endeavor	try
expeditious	fast, quick
facilitate	ease, help
finalize	finish
hopefully	she hoped
impact	effect, change, hit
in conjunction with	with
esthetically challenged	ugly
in regard to	about, on
pertaining to	about, of, on
provide	give, say, supply
retain	keep
therefore, thus	so
and/or	(choose one)
him/her	(choose one)
on or about	(choose one)
etc., et cetera	(don't use)

Don't repeat

Amazing how often corporate writers repeat things, words, ideas, whole phrases. Help me count the ways. Edit these:

```
Fire totally destroyed the facility.

The boss was completely disgusted with the
report.

The auditor was thorough and meticulous.
```

> `Only the CEO alone can authorize the memo with`
> `his signature.`
>
> `Obey all safety rules and regulations current-`
> `ly in effect.`
>
> `The current weather in the city of Houston is`
> `wet and rainy.`

Check your answers with mine.

> `Fire destroyed the men's room.`

Destroyed means *total*. And I can't resist putting *men's room* in place of *facility*. Use *factory*, if you mean *factory*.

> `The boss was disgusted with the report.`

The adverb, *completely*, adds nothing.

> `The auditor was thorough.`

Or *meticulous*. Pick one. Either will do.

> `Only the CEO can sign the memo.`

Only means *alone*. *Authorize with his signature* means *sign*.

> `Obey all safety rules.`

Currently and *in effect* are redundant. You don't need either.

> `It's raining in Houston.`

They must teach this style in airline school. *Wet* repeats *rainy*, which is *weather*, right? You don't need to point out that Houston is a city. Do you? Oh, and only use *current* with electricity; use *now* when you mean now.

Cutting in action

Recall the Army memo in *Chapter 1*. I rewrote the piece, cutting whole grafs. But let's go back to it now and rag on a part of it, using the lessons from this chapter. Take this graf:

> `Specifically, all running landings and autoro-`
> `tation maneuvers terminating with skid-to-`
> `ground contact are suspended until further`
> `notice from this command. Autorotations must`
> `be terminated with full engine recovery BEFORE`
> `fifty (50) feet Above Ground Level (AGL).`
> `Running landings are prohibited altogether,`
> `(altitude notwithstanding and under any cir-`
> `cumstances.)`

Let's edit mainly by cutting.

1. Cut *specifically*. Just say what's suspended.

2. Cut *maneuvers*. You mean autorotations. Learn to recognize all the ways we expand phrases. What is an *out-of-con-*

trol skidding action but a *skid*?

3. Cut *until further notice from this command*. It's in the subject line, remember? Also, recall that near the bottom, the edited memo says: *I will give the all-clear . . .*

4. Change *Autorotations must be terminated with full engine recovery* to active voice to cut words.

5. Cut the *fifty*. Why both words and numerals, for Pete's sake? Hey, if a pilot can't read one, the other is of no value.

6. Same with *Above Ground Level* and *(AGL)*. Use one. I prefer the acronym. If I know my pilots, they will get it. If they don't get it, I need new pilots, eh?

7. Cut *Running landings are prohibited*. It's been said.

8. Cut the phrase, *altogether, (altitude notwithstanding and under any circumstances.)*. Not to be redundant, but that phrase repeats itself over and over again, at least three times.

```
Running landings and autorotations terminating
with skid-to-ground contact are suspended.
Make full engine recovery from autorotations
at 50 feet AGL or higher.
```

9. I'd edit once more, to change the first sentence to the active voice, add a more emphatic verb, and clean up the graf:

```
Stop all running landings and autorotations to
the ground. Make full engine recovery of
autorotations at 50 feet AGL or higher.
```

Seen enough? Questions?

What about technical writing?

Good question.

Some jobs require a technical language all their own. You didn't go to college for eight years and earn a degree in electromagnet engineering just to have a guy like me tell you to stop using the words, *electromagnetic engineering*.

You learned all those high-tech terms that help you talk to other PhDs and you're not about to give them up to some Reading Ease Ideal.

I see your point. Fact is, even my last edit doesn't meet any of the standards except average word length. Too many characters, too many syllables, vocabulary too complex, reading ease, far from ideal. Look here . . .

Reading Ease: Stats of Edited Helo Graf

Microsoft Word	Reading Ease	CCW Ideal
Words per sentence (avg):	10.5	15 maximum
Characters per word (avg):	5	4.5 maximum
Passive voice:	0 %	2% maximum
Flesch Reading Ease:	47.1 %	75% minimum
Flesch-Kincaid Level:	9.2	4-6 or lower

Corel WordPerfect	Reading Ease	CCW Ideal
Words per sentence (avg):	10.5	15 maximum
Syllables per word (avg):	1.8	1.5 maximum
Passive voice:	0 %	2% maximum
Sentence complexity:	4	30 maximum
Vocabulary complexity:	43	15 maximum

Figure 5-2 - Reading ease stats fall short for edited helicopter graf.

The problem? Terms that scuttle reading ease stats:

```
running landings

autorotations (used twice)

engine recovery
```

I was a UH-1H pilot. So I know it doesn't make sense to beat my brains pulpy looking for less technical terms. Pilots get these words and all the concepts behind them.

So now the question is, *How do you handle reading ease?*

You have options. You could ignore the Ideal. You could raise the bar, that is, set a different ideal. You could pad out a paragraph with little words, as in . . .

```
By the way, you can pull a fast one and pad
out a doc so each word is four ltrs or even
two. But don't be dumb, for Pete sake.
```

What's the point of that? Here's a real-world solution.

If you're writing to your peers

With people who use high-tech terms daily, you can assume they will not stumble on them. What you want to know is . . .

What is the reading ease of my text, without the high-tech terms?

Only one way to find out. Replace each high-tech term with a neutral, non-technical word and test your writing.

Let's run such a test on our revised graf after we insert the word *ideal* in place of each high-tech term. You wouldn't get a fair result if you deleted the terms and ran the scan. And you're not likely to find a word with 4.5 characters and 1.5 syllables to meet the characters-per-word ideals of MS Word and Corel WP. *Ideal* is two syllables, five letters. So we didn't cheat the test in rounding up to arrive at . . .

```
Stop all ideal and ideal to the ground. Make
full ideal of ideal at 50 feet AGL or higher.
```

I admit, it looks a bit goofy. But it will give us a fair test of our CC Writer Ideal standards. It will tell us our reading ease after we control for unique, high-tech terms. The result . . .

Reading Ease: Controlling for Hi-Tech Terms

Microsoft Word	Before	After	CCW Ideal
Words per sentence (avg):	10.5	9.5	15 maximum
Characters per word (avg):	5	3.6	4.5 maximum
Passive voice:	0%	0%	2% maximum
Flesch Reading Ease:	47.1%	85.8%	75% minimum
Flesch-Kincaid Level:	9.2	3.6	4-6 or lower

Corel WordPerfect	Before	After	CCW Ideal
Words per sentence (avg):	10.5	9.5	15 maximum
Syllables per word (avg):	1.8	1.36	1.5 maximum
Passive voice:	0%	0%	2% maximum
Sentence complexity:	4	2	30 maximum
Vocabulary complexity:	43	0	15 maximum

Figure 5-3 - Edited helicopter graf, controlled for high-tech terms.

You can see the effect at a glance. The drop in cpw in Word yielded two huge leaps in reading ease in both Flesch and Flesch-Kincaid. In WP we got two huge drops, in syllables per word and in vocabulary complexity.

One last questions. Did the word *ideal* cheat the scales?

Let's check. Let's run the original graf before any edit, then insert *ideal* for the same high-tech terms, and run it again.

Helo Graf: Controlling for Hi-Tech Terms

Microsoft Word	Before	After	CCW Ideal
Words per sentence (avg):	15.3	14.3	15 maximum
Characters per word (avg):	6.6	6.1	4.5 maximum
Passive voice:	66 %	66 %	2% maximum
Flesch Reading Ease:	1.8 %	17 %	75% minimum
Flesch-Kincaid Level:	12	12	4-6 or lower

Corel WordPerfect	Before	After	CCW Ideal
Words per sentence (avg):	15.3	14.3	15 maximum
Syllables per word (avg):	2.32	2.16	1.5 maximum
Passive voice:	100 %	100 %	2% maximum
Sentence complexity:	11	9	30 maximum
Vocabulary complexity:	80	76	15 maximum

Figure 5-4 - Stats for original helicopter graf, before and after testing.

There you have it. Proof that the word *ideal* barely nudged the stats. Our edits carried the freight in getting to standards.

CAUTION: Copy your file before you inject the word *ideal*. Work in the copy so you don't mess up the original.

If you're writing to non-tech types

Use acronyms when you can, as in *portfolio diversification (PD)* in that sentence a few pages back. We cut it to *PD* and boosted our reading ease. Write the high-tech term the first time you need it, followed by the acronym in parentheses. After that, just use the acronym. That's the best you can do.

Chapter summary

Cut big words down to size.

6

Focus your edit on writing short, tight sentences

Keep to a single idea in a sentence. Be brief, as in these
next five chapters. Break fat sentences in two. Readers find
it easier to follow your logic when you stick to that Ideal of no
more than an average 15 words per sentence.

The period is your friend

I write short sentences. You already know that. What you
don't know is, this chapter will be over soon after you turn
the page. The Ideal of 15 words per sentence is so easy to
meet. A long boring sentence of 39 words reads easier when
you break it up. Even if the new sentences are just as boring.
Simply plug in some periods.

Here, I'll prove it with this yawner from the Army memo:

```
Once pending skid MWOs have been applied (and
adequately tested by competent authority as
designated by this headquarters or higher),
the aforementioned procedures may be resumed,
but once again, only by this command, on
notice exclusively from the undersigned.
```

The vital stats are: one sentence, and 39 words. Now let's
put in two periods and add the minor changes we need to keep
the sense of this senseless blather.

> Once pending skid MWOs have been applied (and
> adequately tested by competent authority as
> designated by this headquarters or higher),
> the aforementioned procedures may be resumed.
> But once again, only by this command. On
> notice exclusively from the undersigned.

What happened?

In MS Word

We get 5.5 characters per word (in WP, too, of course). But we go from 11 percent on the Flesch Reading Ease Scale to 37 percent, and we drop from 12+ on Flesch-Kincaid to 11.2. Nothing to brag about, but a gain still.

In Corel WP

We still get two syllables per word in both versions. The 70 on vocabulary complexity stays the same. But we see a drop from 65 on sentence complexity to 21, within our Ideal.

Is this a simple numbers gain (game)?

No. It's a gain in reading ease. Because the period is a firm stop. Insert a period after a single idea, and the reader pauses a second. Your idea hits her between the left and right brain.

Read that paragraph again. Then read this next one:

No, the period is a firm stop, meaning that if you insert a period after a single idea, the reader pauses a second, and your idea hits her between the left and right brain.

See how the comma is a soft stop? See how the long sentence keeps stringing you along, a literal train of thought, one boxcar phrase hitched to the next with commas?

Combine this editing tip with others until you get all five Ideals to fall into line. Then you'll boost your work into the realm of the truly Creative Corporate Writer.

Bonus tip. In high-tech writing, keep your sentences simple to get high reading ease, even with lay readers.

Chapter summary

Cut your sentences down to size. Use periods to set off ideas. Then combine this editing trick with the others.

7

Focus your edit on writing just one topic in each paragraph

You can help reading ease by breaking your writing into short paragraphs, one topic to each graf.

Lighten up

Forget reading ease stats for a sec. Hold this book open at arm's length. Take in both pages. Feel your eyes drift to this page, which just *looks* easier to read.

White space helps reading ease

Novelists use white space in dialogue to speed up the pace. News writers avoid dense stories. They use white space.

CC Writers write short grafs by grouping sentences that pertain to a single topic. When in doubt, they add a return.

They also use . . .

- Bullets like this to highlight main points
- Bold headlines to help readers skim
- Graphics to support their main points

Chapter summary

Write short paragraphs, each with a single idea.

8

Focus your edit on writing in a polite, informal style

You boost reading ease when you connect with your reader on a personal level. So, CC Writer, use an easy style. Say please and thank you. Write as casually as you can. Be genuine. Please.

Please lighten up, thank you

Good morning. Here's a rule of thumb. Outfit your writing in casual dress. Keep it as informal as you can without giving offense.

I've lived up to this notion in this book. I've used a light but not flippant tone. Okay, not *too* flippant. Still, if you've made it this far, we're practically pals.

What's the trick to a polite, informal style? No trick, just the tips I gave you in the previous chapters. Let's review them.

Cut to the chase — it's polite to put your bottom line up top so readers don't have to either guess at it or hunt for it.

Write to a single name and face —you are more casual than if you write to the faceless masses.

Use the CC Writer's Ideal — it boosts informal writing.

Use short words and sentences — They say, *I'm thinking of your needs, gentle reader. It's all about YOU.*

Next, look at this brief list, the . . .

7 habits of highly effective, polite, informal CC Writers

1. Use *you*, the second-person form of address

2. Use *I*, the first-person

3. Say *please* and *thank you*, even if you're the boss — it's no sign of weakness to be polite

4. Write contractions, like *I'll*, *you're*, and so on

5. Write the way you speak — to achieve this, read your writing aloud, into a tape recorder, and play it back

6. Ask questions to engage your *You*. Give answers so she can compare her opinion to yours — too easy, huh?

7. Invent — I've invented words like *speakina* in *speakina which* to engage your wit, and *graf*, a journalism term that boosts reading ease. But do be wary when you invent at work. It's too easy to get too cute.

Avoid phony courtesy

The corporate world is full of baloney-phrases that I refuse to use. I never write *Sincerely yours*. I'm married and I'll never be yours. I don't even use *Dear* to greet somebody, unless it's one of my kids. Don't be thanking me *in advance for your kind consideration*. Unless you're handing out sick bags, too.

I do write *Good morning* . . . as a greeting.

And I often close with . . .

Best . . . .

Chapter summary

Polite, informal writing is one of the tools of the Creative Corporate Writer. It shows style. And it's based on the sound principles of the basic 10 Suggestions of the CC Writer. Thank you.

9

Focus your reader
with stories and pictures

The Creative Corporate Writer knows that some readers get more out of writing when pictures, tables, charts, and graphics illustrate his points. So he uses them. Most readers love a good story. So he tells stories.

Paint pictures with both words and graphics

In a fiction writers workshop I taught in Delaware last year, I told my audience that I would not bore them with war stories of my fight to break in as a novelist.

But soon I heard myself telling about how one publisher rejected me not once, but twice, on the same submission. Oh, insult, oh, injury.

The first note felt like that *Peanuts* cartoon strip in which Snoopy reads a form rejection: "Dear Author, just a reminder — you can send junk mail via fourth-class postage."

The second letter killed me with its kindness. The editor wrote words like *compelling, well-written, jumps with energy.* But the ending wasn't much better than a form letter.

"Sorry, but we don't publish fiction like this," the editor wrote. "Send it to a house like Avon, Bantam, or Dell."

I checked my log. Yep, I'd sent the novel to all three. And

yep, all three had rejected it. So I crept off to weep in my beer.

Until next morning. When I awoke with a start. *Good grief,
Charlie Brown!* That editor had just written the most encouraging words I'd ever heard.

So I copied the letter. I sent it to all houses three with a brief
pitch note: *Wanna take a look at a compelling novel? Don't
take my word for it. Look what this editor wrote.*

Bob Mecoy at Dell said yes and published *Beastmaker*, a
thriller about cloning gone wrong, to great fanfare.

Do you believe it? I sold my first novel using a rejection letter as a calling card.

Later, I sold my rejection story to *Writer's Digest* magazine.

And I closed my first Writer's Digest book, *You Can Write
a Novel*, with it.

As I said, I also used it in my workshop last year. A guy
came up at the first break and said, "Tell more war stories. We
want to hear how real people can break in."

So I'm telling it again right here. That's a lot of mileage for
one story, eh? More to the point . . .

Are you still with me, still hooked by it?

Of course you are. Everybody loves a story about the underdog who breaks into a dog-eat-dog industry.

Get my point? Remember the Geek story? Jill and *The
Three Bears*? Dylan saying: "Tell a story about me." The Bell
Curve? The Aiming Tool? Word lists? Reading Ease charts?

I rest my case. Thumb into this book. See how the stories
and pictures jump out? Use names, places, facts, figures, real-world detail and a bit of wit. Stories and pictures work.

But can you tell a story in a memo? Absolutely. Say you
want to jump-start your sales staff with some new ideas. Start
out with: *You can even sell with rejection. I know of one
author who . . . .*

Chapter summary

Tell stories. Use pictures, charts, and tables to brighten your
reader's day by making your writing easy to understand.

10

Focus – Organize for clarity

You already ID'd your bottom line and made it the top line. Now identify your main points and put a logic to them, a logic your reader can follow. Use one or more of the five styles in this chapter and the tips that clarify even further.

Logic by the numbers

Notice how I avoid the word, *outline*? Corporate writers hate *outline* almost as much as *grammar*. So I don't use it.

So let's just get organized, shall we? In our writing.

Say you already have your bottom line. You've already made it your top line. How do you tell the rest of your story?

Simple. List your main points. Some word programs have a feature that lets you shuffle points. It's called the (shudder) *outline* view. If you prefer hard copy, use three-by-five cards and write one idea per. Better yet, use business cards.

In today's economy, every company has a million or so cards in vacant desks of laid-off workers. On the bright side, if you earned a promotion, you earned new cards with your new title. So use the backs of your old cards.

After you write one idea on each card, lay them out in a vertical pattern. Put your bottom line at the top of the row, of course. Shuffle the others below that until you get your order.

Let's talk about some ways to organize for clarity. I'll give you examples as I go.

Alphabetical

I won't insult you with a how-to on this one. Notice how I set up this list in that way, though.

Chronological

Literally, logic in order of time. Suppose you're the owner of a diner who wants to write a memo to your first chef. You begin: *At 4 a.m., heat water to a boil. No later than 5 a.m. add filet mignon to poach for six hours.*

Narrative

You tell a story with a beginning, a middle and an end. Oh, and a point. Entire business books have been written in fable form. *The One Minute Manager*, for one. And *Who Moved My Cheese?* for another. I used this style in the Geek story. Chapter 9 is pure narrative.

Procedural

Organize by telling how a process should work. Or give your reader a clear lesson in how-to. As in, *First do this, then that*. Notice that this style went into the chef story, too.

Recall the section on how to set up MS Word to check reading ease stats. That's procedural.

CAUTION: If you tell a person how to assemble an F-16 fighter aircraft, be sure you test your instructions first. Ask your best friend to try to put the F-16 together to see if your system will fly.

Structural

Here you tell the way the parts in a system fit together. For instance, you might describe the wiring diagram that shows your company's departments and executive structure.

Tips for getting crystal clarity

Don't get hung up on this issue of organizing. Once you have your bottom line, a short piece will write itself. Even so, I have a few ideas to help you get the most from your writing.

Use the Executive Summary

For long pieces, write a brief capsule and put it up front. Be sure to include your bottom line in it. I used an executive summary for this book to . . .

- Appeal to *You*
- Tell the bottom line of *The Creative Corporate Writer*
- Show page numbers for my best stuff
- Sell this book
- This bullet is out of place

Use bullets

When you use bullets as I just did, keep to a style. See how the first four items begin with verbs. They tell you how I used an executive summary to *Appeal, Tell, Show*, and *Sell*. The fifth bullet hits you with a jolt, doesn't it? The topic is wrong, and the style falls apart. Without a lead-off verb, it clunks.

Go back into this book. See how each bullet list holds to style. It might begin with a verb. Or a noun. In each list, the style holds true from top to bottom.

Preview and summarize

Each chapter in this book so far does both. A preview to each chapter helps you see what is to come. A summary tells you what you should get out of the chapter.

Use lots of bold type

If your readers want to skim your main points, make it easy for them. Take this page for example. Start at the top and skim only the bold headlines. See the continuity?

You can preview or review the page at a glance. If you want more detail, you can dip into any segment that appeals to you.

If you wanted to, you could preview this book in a matter of seconds by reading the *Contents* page. In a matter of minutes you could get the gist of my system by reading only the first page of each chapter and the bold type. In only 30 minutes you could start using the Creative Corporate Writer Reading Ease Ideal. In an hour you'd know how to edit your work. Why, in a day—

Forgive me. I do go on. I have a point, though. That graf is my way of showing you one way to . . .

Use an internal summary now and then

I used a graf to tell you how to skim this book. I gave you a fresh angle on my logic to organizing for clarity. This graf is also an internal summary. Of the last segment.

Use clear-cut transitions

I try to keep up a flow in my writing. I want to keep you posted at all times about where we're going in this book. So I often refer to where we've been. I merge one point into another. It helps you read. It gives you the feeling of a fast pace.

For instance, look at the many times I used the dot-dot-dot thing (. . .) to end one graf and flow my thought into the next heading. You could argue, as several editors have, that I over-use the device. Hey, you get no argument from me. In any case . . .

Here's a list of ways to transition:

- Use the dot-dot-dot thing, but don't over-use it

- Try transition words that carry an idea from one phrase to another: *So, for instance, in conclusion, finally, that way, by the way, later, next morning, first, second, third*

- Repeat words to reflect from one segment of a piece to another, for instance, the word, flow, reflects from the first graf in this segment to the second graf

- Reflect ideas from one graf to the next to sweep the reader along, such as in this graf, which reflects back to every previous point in this segment

Give a clear-cut conclusion

Don't be coy about it. If you must, use the blunt words, *In conclusion . . . .*

A conclusion, even if it's a mere summary, tells that you know you had a point in writing. Then when you can . . .

Recommend

When you can. A conclusion wraps up your logic. A recommendation shows you have the courage to state your position. It gives your reader a straw man to use in setting her own stance. If you offer choices, pick the one you like and recommend it.

By the way, put your recommendation into the executive summary, too. That way, a reader doesn't have to guess where you're coming from when he reads your piece.

In conclusion, I give you this . . .

Chapter summary

Organize for clarity by using one or more of the five systems of logic: alphabetical, chronological, narrative, procedural, and structural. Try all eight tips to get to crystal clarity.

The Creative Corporate Writer's bag of 101 tricks

I'll use the rest of this book to lay out tips that will help you write with more clarity. It's stuff that didn't fit well into the other chapters. Many points came out of my editing lessons for the salary and Army memos. I want to address these points without the clutter of early chapters. Oh, and I admit it, some of them are just pet peeves. In the interest of fairness, I'll mark those with an asterisk, as in . . .

* Avoid multiple exclamation points!!!!!

* Avoid even single exclamation points!
Except for a true exclamation, like *Rats!* Or *Cubs win!*

DON'T WRITE HEADLINES IN ALL-CAPS
They're too hard to read

Don't write all-caps to emphasize body text, either
It reads like shouting. AND WHY WOULD YOU SHOUT?

Its is possessive

While *it's* is the contraction of *it is*

Don't overuse adjectives

Prefer active, living verbs and concrete nouns.

Avoid *per,* as in *per your memo*
Other than uses like *words per sentence*, let cats per.

Don't sweat the small stuff like clichés
In one sense, clichés boost reading ease because they are so familiar you don't even stop to read them. I don't like clichés. But I don't go Frank Costanza on them, either. I like to wring a new wrinkle from them. Easy as 3.1416, eh? (Easy as pi.)

Avoid awful alliteration, word strings starting with the same letter

Use the search function to find *-ly* words, adverbs
In your word program, select *Find*, search for *ly*, check each adverb ending in *-ly* to see if it can be cut.

Search for *-ize* and *-ization* and cut those when you can

Search for *-tion* words, too, and cut them down to size

Affect is a verb meaning *to influence*

Effect as a verb means *to produce*

Effect is most often a noun, meaning *the result produced*

Impact is a noun not a verb
WRONG: *The 10-pound report impacted him a lot.*
RIGHT: *The impact of the 10-pound report broke his ribs, his spirit, and his momentum up the career ladder.*

* Don't *entitle* songs, books, reports, or films — *title* them
Entitle refers to *ownership.* I *titled* this book: *The Creative Corporate Writer.* I'm *entitled* to its copyright.

Don't *type up* or *print out*; *type* and *print* will do the job

Avoid writing *he/she*; use one

Avoid *and/or* — choose one

Don't use *et cetera* or *etc.*

* Avoid the expression *and much, much more* in sales copy

It usually means: *I got nothing more. Zip. Nada. Nil.*

Momento? Maybe in Spanish; you mean *memento*

* *Loan* is a noun, dang it, a noun; *lend* is the verb — always

You *lend* money. That money is a *loan.*

* Use *hopefully* the way you use a gun

Carefully. If you don't know how to handle it, leave it alone. Here's a memory aid. You wouldn't say, *Hopefully you will die.* Even when you mean, *It is hoped you will die.* You might say, *I hope you die.* Which still pales next to, *Drop dead.* If you insist on *hopefully*, try, *Hopefully, I give you this poison.*

Use *fewer* with things you can count, *less than* with quantities

He has fewer than 10 fingers and less than enough sense.

Imply means *to suggest*

Whereas *infer* means to *deduce*

Your is possessive

You're is the contraction of *you are*

Their is possessive

They're is the contraction of *they are*

There is the pronoun, as in *over there*

Don't modify *unique* with *very, more,* or *so* — *unique* is unique

Don't get too *excited*

Avoid the word in sales copy and executive memos. When you write in the newsletter, *We're excited about our audit!* I'm thinking, *What does the IRS know?*

If you're truly *excited,* you're *eager* not *anxious*

Memory aid: *anxious* refers to *anxiety.*

Avoid being *in close proximity to*; you're *near*

Avoid *disseminating*

It could lead to a sexual harassment suit. While we're at it, *artificial dissemination* might result in paternity questions.

Currently means *now;* use *now*

Don't string nouns together as adjectives

As in *emergency procedure qualification flights*. What the writer meant was *check rides*.

Avoid *unforeseen* and *unforeseeable*

What you mean is, *Oops, I never saw that coming*.

Catastrophic mishap really means *crash*

Accident usually means *crash*

Avoid *previously mentioned;* just re-mention the issue; or not

Same with *aforementioned*

Accommodations? Do you mean *lodging* or *hotel room?*

Or do your *accommodations* mean *aids to the disabled?*

Watch out for *activity*

It's often a sneak-attack of redundancy. It's not a *sports activity*; it's a *sport. Thunderstorm activity* is one or more *storms*.

Same deal with *event*

A *snow event* or a *blizzard?* Which would you choose?

Advance plan? Why not a simple *plan?*

Same with *future planning* (What good is *retro-planning?*)

Rather? Avoid using it as a qualifier

Rather pretty? Not unless you mean Dan the news man.

Avoid *very* as a qualifier, too

Writers use *very* and *rather* because they're too lazy to look up a precise word. *Rather* sounds pompous besides. (Dan, the news man, pompous? You be the judge.)

* Write *Canada goose*, not *Canadian goose*

You *center on*, not *center around*

At this point in time, put simply, means *now*

* It's *nuclear (new-clear)*, not *new-cue-lerr*

I know, it's not a writing problem. It's a pet peeve. Be nice if we elected a president who could pronounce the word.

* *By the same token* — say it if you like, but never write it

Don't use parentheses willy-nilly (Do as I say, not as I do)

Say *purchase* if you like, but write *buy* for the verb

Criterion is singular, *criteria* refers to more than one *criterion*

Same deal with *media* — It's *The media are jackals*

* It's the *Medal of Honor*

Not the *Congressional Medal of Honor*.

Quality is a noun, not an adjective

A *quality* product? No, a *high-quality* product. Or *low*.

A *joint collaboration* is a redundant *collaboration*

Or perhaps the sharing of an illegal substance.

Avoid *however* in your writing

However seems hokey to me. Worse, it tempts you to string clauses together, making your writing bulky.

Ditto *importantly* and *more importantly*

Ditto *in addition to* and *moreover*

If you don't use a term when you talk, be wary about using it when you write. Don't go politician on your reader.

Prohibited altogether isn't any more prohibited than *prohibited*

Adequately tested? As opposed to *inadequately tested*?

Mid-air collision? Where is mid-air? You mean *in-flight*

As to *collision,* use *crash* when you can

Notoriety is not the same as *fame*

Notoriety is ill-fame. Use it only with bad guys and deeds.

Ditto *infamous*; remember Dec.7? A day that lives in *infamy?*

Don't write *thus* and *thusly*

Verily, for thusly, you do not come off rather stuffily.

Vast is a great word, but it doesn't go well with *difference*

Sounds as if you're stretching the facts. Oh, and why not be
the first writer in memory to write *wasteland* without *vast?*

For the purpose of has no purpose; say *to*

Interface with is a rotten substitute for *talk to*

End result? No, *result*

The *result* of using *end result?* You don't sound as smart as
you're trying to sound. Mentally, your readers correct you.

Don't *commence, begin*

And for Pete's sake, don't *commence to begin.*

* Same with *proceed*

One best-selling novelist is fond of writing, *She proceeded
to ask* . . . . He means, *She asked* . . . .

* Watch what you *make,* you could be making verbs into nouns

Don't *make corrections* to the report. Just *correct* it.

Say *provide,* if you like, but write *give*

Don't *award with a prize,* or even a plaque

The CEO *gives the sales award to him.* She doesn't *award
him with a prize.* She's *awarding* the prize and rewarding him.

Same deal with *present with*

Gild the lily? Nope. *Gild gold* and *paint the lily*

Or so Shakespeare said.

Each and every? Nah, pick one (*not one or the other*)

It's *different from*, not *different than*

Gather together? Why not simply *gather*?

*Free gift?

Permit me to steal a line from the song *Me and Bobby McGee*, but a gift *ain't worth nothin if it ain't free*.

En route is two words; it's not *enroute*

Don't use *individual* for *person*

And please don't write the redundant *one individual*

If and when? Use either *if* or *when*

And not *either/or*, please — pick one

I hate to say this

Then don't.

Ditto, *It goes without saying*

Funny thing happened to me on the way here

Don't write this into your speech and don't say it, either. I'll bet it's no more funny than . . .

That reminds me of a funny story . . .

Which always reminds me to set the snooze alarm.

Minimize works

Maximize doesn't

Whether or not? Nope, just *whether*

I would like to tell you about a new development

Don't write whether you'd like to tell. Just tell it. And, oh, I've never heard of an *old development*, except in the slums.

Ditto with *I would like to introduce*

I'm going to means *I will*, so write, *I will*

In the coming year means *next year*

In the current year means this year

All together now, speak these words aloud: *I will become a Creative Corporate Writer this year.*

By the way, if you're counting, that's more than 101 tips. Here's another bonus . . .

A few spelling tips

Accommodation is a big word, so it takes two *C*s, two *M*s

Alot? Nope, you mean *a lot*

Alright is wrong, too; you mean *all right*

Bizarre how many ways *bizarre* can be misspelled

Embarrass, with two *R*s but . . .

Harass with one

Judgement? No, *judgment*, one *E*

Occur has two *C*s one *R*, and occurred has two *C*s and two *R*s

Separate, not *seperate*

Souvenir, not *souvenier*

Receive, not *recieve*; the rule is *I before E, except after C*

Yield; again, *I before E*, but *weird, E before I*

Weird, huh?

Enough with the spelling. Use the spell-check.

A Final Word (or Three)

Okay, several words, on three topics. Three mega-tips. Do them and you will write ten times better. Now get busy. And good luck.

1. Dismiss the idea of writer's block

It doesn't exist. You're just lazy. Or else you have no passion for the project. Get over the romantic notion of writer's block. Ever heard of brain surgeon's block? Airline pilot's block? Of course not. Why should writers get a mythic disease to use as an excuse not to work?

How to motivate yourself if you're lazy? That is the question. Answer? Try these final two suggestions:

2. Focus. When all else fails, focus on the task at hand

Put aside all else. As the motivational speakers say:

> Do what needs to be done, when it needs to be done, whether you want to do it or not.

3. Begin

Write. Run a reading ease scan. Edit until you meet all five ideals. The system will absorb you. You will get done.

Congratulations! You are the Creative Corporate Writer.

Index

101 tricks, 101
15-Second Deadline, 17, 26
15 seconds to the bottom line, 25
7 habits of highly effective writers, 92
Aiming tool, the Creative Corporate Writer's, 44
Acronyms, 86
Active voice, 75, 83
Add document command in WordPerfect, 67
Adjectives, 102
Adverbs, 80
All-caps, 101
Alphabetical organizing, 96
Amuse, writing to, 31, 43, 44
Amusing, dramatizing, entertaining, diverting, 43
Army memo, 19
Army memo, revised, 21
Atomic Flyswatters, 80
Author bio, 112
Authors, best-selling in reading ease study, 74-75
Averages in WordPerfect, 68
Basic counts in WordPerfect, 68
Bears, The Three, 33
Belkin, Lisa, 30
Bell curve showing Creative Corporate Writers, 9
Bell curve showing student grades, 9
Belkin, Lisa, 31
Bernstein, Theodore M., 80
Bold headlines to help readers, 89
Bold type, 97
Bottom Line, 26, 17, 21, 23, 24, 28, 41, 82
— putting into the subject line, 26
— as topmost, 26
Brevity, 22

Bulletproof, 23
Bullets, 97
Bureaucratese, 81
Characters per word, 54, 76
Characters, 52
Chronological organizing, 96
Clarity, tips for getting crystal, 97
Cliches, 102
Clinton, President Bill, 34, 35
Coincidence, 30
Comparison document, 66 — 68
Compel, 17, 19, 22, 43, 44
Compelling by ordering, persuading, selling, 42
Compelling — The Road to Best-selling, 2
Competition, 8
Conclusion, reasons to write a clear-cut, 99
Consultations, 2
Contents, 5
Contractions, 92
Conversational, 24
Copy-and-paste jargon, 24
Corel WordPerfect, 58
Creative Corporate Writer's Ideal, 92
— elements of, 75
— the key to
— secret to, 31
Creative Corporate Writers, 10
Cutting, 82-83
Deadline, 25
dot-dot-dot device, 98
Eclipse, 31
Editing results of, 77
Eureka, 32
Executive summary, this book's, 1
— using, 97
Falk, Ruma, 32,

Final word, 109
Flagged issues in WordPerfect, 68-69
Flesch, 57, 76, 85
Flesch-Kincaid, 57, 58, 74, 76, 85
— in WordPerfect, 68
Focus, 7, 11, 12, 60
— lack of, 11
— when all else fails, 109
Force Recon, 76
Gaak, 31, 32
Geek, 31
Grammar & style options in MS Word, 62
Grammar, 14, 15, 95
— rules, 12
Grammatik, for reading ease stats on a PC, 66
Graphics, 93
— to support main points, 89
Ground Zero, 30
Helicopter Memo, before, 19-21
Hierarchy of Needs, 32
Hot button, 29, 35, 37, 41
How The Mind Works, 30
Ideal, Creative Corporate Writer's, 59
Inform, 22, 44
— by warning, advising, educating, 42
Index, 111
Informal writing, 24
It's All about Me, 36
King, Stephen, 36
Let's Talk about Me, 34
Let's Talk about You, 34, 35, 36
Literary Genius, 12
Literary prose, 14
-ly words, 80
Maslow, Abraham F., 32-33
Mecoy, Bob, 94
Microsoft Word, 58, 74

— setting up to run reading ease scales, 60
Misspellings, common, 108
Mother Teresa, 37
Murphy, Dylan James, 33
Narrative as a way of organizing, 96
Needs, Hierarchy of, 32
New York Times Magazine, 30
One-minute pre-writing job-aid, 45
Organizing, 96
— alphabetical
— chronological
— narrative
— procedural
— structural
Passive sentences, 54
Passive voice, 76, 78
— explained, 54-57
— settings, 62
— in WordPerfect, 68
— pitfalls of, 56-57
— changing to active, effect on reading ease, 77
Pentagon, 30
Picture, screen — see Screen picture
Pictures, 93
Pompous words, 79
Procedural organizing, 96
Punctuation to improve reading keys, 87-88
Questions, asking, to engage a reader, 92
Phony courtesy, 92
Readability scales, 57
Readability statistics setup,
63-64
Reading comprehension diagram, 53
Reading ease, 51, 57, 89, 91
— in technical writing, 85
Reading Ease Ideal, 60
— for novelists, 75-76
— discovery of, 74
— statistics of Chapter i, 70
Recommendation, why to write one, 99
References, 26
Reflecting ideas, to transition, 99
Repeating words or forms of words, to transition, 98
Salary Memo, after, 13
Salary Memo, before, 12-13
Sales Talk, All Talk Is, 36-37
Screen picture setup on the Mac, 64-65
— on the PC using Windows, 66
—how to take, 64
Seminars, 2
Sentence complexity, 59
Sentence length, 76
Sept. 11, 2001, 29-30, 34
Simplicity, 52
Single reader, 39
— You, 41
Strategic pages, 1
Structural organizing, 96
Subject Line, 26-27
— tips for writing 27
Summary, chapter 97
Summary, executive — see Executive summary
Summary, internal, 98
Syllables per word, 54, 85-86
Synonyms for said, 80
Technical writing, 83
Cut to the chase, 17
The 10 Suggestions listed: Contents, 5, 11-12
The Fiction Writer's Brainstormer, 2, 74, 75
The Three Bears, 33
Pinker, Stephen, 30
-tion words, 79, 80
Transition words, 98
Transitions, 98
Twin Towers, 30
Vocabulary complexity, 59, 86
Volcano and The Virgin story, 31
What this book can do for you, 7
White space, 89
Word count, 52
Wordiness, 63
WordPerfect, reading ease stats in, 66
Words per sentence, 52
Workshops, 2
World Trade Center, 30
Writer's block, 109
Writers Digest magazine, 94
You Can Write a Novel, 2
You, 7, 29
— the company, 8
— the person, 7
Zee End

About the Author

James V. Smith, Jr. is a professional speaker and workshop presenter, teaching his Creative Corporate Writer system in the workplace.

He is the author of more than a dozen books in fiction and nonfiction, including *You Can Write a Novel* and *The Fiction Writer's Brainstormer* and the *Force Recon* and *Delta Force* (2004) novels from Berkley Publishing. He was a reporter for *The Dallas Morning News* and *The Indianapolis News* as well as a four-time national award-winning columnist. He is a former Army officer, helicopter pilot, and director of DoD's Journalism Department. His clients include Arthur Andersen, Arvin, the King County (Seattle area) Library System, The Lilly Endowment, Lockheed Martin, and Safeco. He is a Writer's Digest national workshop presenter. He has written and designed books for other national speakers.